The author with young friend.

Adirondack Album BY BARNEY FOWLER

Herewith presented Volume 3 of Adirondack Album. It continues presentation of an unusual view of New York State's giant Adirondack region and its fringes by a reporter-photographer of more than a half century experience in the newspaper field.

"I love to hear water running over stones, a woman with a low voice singing, a loon on a moonlit night, a partridge drumming in the fall, a hound dog after a rabbit, a robin just before a storm."

—— *Ira Gray*

Printed by Benche, Inc.
31 Lafayette Street
Schenectady, N.Y. 12301

Typesetting by Silverline Composition Service
40 Broadway Extension
Amsterdam, N.Y. 12010

ISBN
0-9605556-2-5

Contents

As of this writing we are nearing the 100th anniversary of the New York State Forest Preserve. This, Volume No. 3 of the Adirondack Album series, makes due note of that fact and the author fervently hopes that throughout the state there will be ceremonies in 1985 commemorating the bold move of creation.

Because Volume 1 and Volume 2 have met with gratifying success (and are still available) the Album format is relatively unchanged. The paper has been chosen to eliminate "bounceback," or glare and is New York State made.

The style is casual for easy and relaxing reading. The pages remain eight-and-one half by eleven inches for better display of photographs; the type remains 11 pt. Press Roman medium and captions are in 10 pt Press Roman Italics. There is reason. Larger type eliminates eye strain.

Introduction

The thought occurred in writing this introduction to Volume 3 of the Adirondack Album series that I would remiss to a startling degree if mention were not made of legislation which not only changed the physical structure of a great portion of New York State, but made the state into a model for others to follow.

Many today take the Adirondack Park for granted.

It was not always so.

The pillage began in the 1700's when millions of furs were harvested in the mountains for home use and for shipping to foreign lands.

Then came the axe and saw. Throughout much of the 1800's the timbered lands were cut savagely; untold billions of mature trees were felled, sawed and the lumber shipped to all parts of the world. Hundreds of sawmills came into being. In some cases when a mill was offered for sale it was stipulated in the advertisement that there rested around the mill an "inexhaustible" supply of timber. Foolish words and untrue. Nothing in Nature is inexhaustible. Consider the passenger pigeon, now extinct. Consider also the beech tree which is dying off as substantial growth because of a blight. The elm is another sad and classic example.

In days gone by rivers and streams were dammed to float the timber to sawmills. Vast areas were flooded in so doing. Fish life suffered. So did animal life. We have tragedy of another form striking us today — acid rain. Laws called a halt to the former. Perhaps the courage to institute laws against the latter will solve that problem. We can hope. We can pray.

There was a wild abandon in the North Country where fortunes existed for the taking. Reforestation was a nasty word; areas which were lumbered became eroded to bedrock. Few stands of "virgin" timber remain today. The reasons for their presence are many. One was inaccessibility. Another was economic consideration. Others were prohibitions by private owners who wished to preserve. And still another was the fact that law moved in to protect our watersheds.

Hundreds of miles of railroads, constructed for use in the logging industry, carried not only logs but fire; locomotives scattered sparks and hundreds of thousands of timberland acres were burned into blackened wastelands. Evidence of early fires is still visible today in charred and decaying stumps.

It was not until 1885 that constitutional protection of a sort was offered state lands. The Forest Preserve came into being. The Forest Commission was created. The preserve was defined as "all lands now owned or that may hereafter be acquired by the state of New York within the counties of Clinton (except the towns of Altona and Dannemora), Essex, Franklin, Fulton, Hamilton, Herkimer, Lewis, Saratoga, St. Lawrence, Warren, Washington, Greene, Ulster and Sullivan, shall constitute the Forest Preserve."

It was specified that lands constituting the preserve would not be sold, nor would they be leased or taken by any corporation. They were to be kept as wild forest.

Note in the creation of the preserve that Greene, Ulster and Sullivan Counties were mentioned; these are well south of the Adirondacks. This bears explanation.

The North Country has its own "continental divide," that is, where watersheds meet and streams flow their respective courses. This photo taken where Rt. 28 enters the Blue Mt. Lake area; as noted, the St. Lawrence River and the Hudson River watersheds are those involved, the St. Lawrence to the north, Hudson's River receiving water flowing southward.

When we speak of the Forest Preserve, we speak of public ownership and protection today of 2,310,000 acres in the Adirondacks, and 265,000 acres in the Catskills area. Too often, in discussion of the preserve, the Catskill region becomes a conversational orphan.

Obviously the preserve has grown from year to year. But it wasn't always easy. In 1885, for instance, the legislature was asked for one million dollars to buy forest lands. Only $15,000 was appropriated! Today in some areas that amount wouldn't be sufficient to buy

State marker, self explanatory, was photographed in the Perkins Clearing area north of Speculator. Area was scene of considerable lumbering activity during World War Two by International Paper Co. It is believed the chain saw, as we know it today, was first used in the Adirondacks in this section.

enough land for a fox to roam. Since the Northway and other highways came into being land values have risen sharply.

What one might call strict constitutional protection did not come until 1894 when the famous "forever wild" clause was formulated. This read at first:

"The lands of the state, now owned or hereinafter acquired, constituting the Forest Preserve as fixed by law, shall be forever kept as wild forest lands. They shall not be leased, sold or exchanged or be taken by any corporation, public or private, nor shall the timber thereon be sold or removed."

A judge, William P. Goodelle, Syracuse, was astute enough to note an omission. He wanted the word "destroyed" added. It was. So the phrase read: "sold or removed or destroyed."

(This prevented the destruction of trees by man-made flooding. It should be remembered that private tracts often adjoined state-owned ones).

The designation "Adirondack Park" came into being in May, 1892, and it was then that the so-called "blue line," or boundary, was devised. At one time this line could have become reality.

A state legislator wanted the blue line actually painted in that color — on boundary trees! The suggestion died without glory.

Have conditions developed for the better? Today, despite past pillage, the U.S. Forestry Service's preliminary report on new timber inventory shows that New York ranks first among northeastern states in forested acres. The figure is incredible; even more so is the report that sixty percent of the state's land is now covered by forests! Obviously this includes a great deal of private holdings which can and are being lumbered.

The old days are long gone when the Big Boom at Glens Falls saw two millions logs floated down Hudson's River and its tributaries, the annual harvest from the Adirondacks. The last of the big logs came down the river in 1924; the last pulp load was driven by Finch-Pruyn in the spring of 1950. An era ended. At one time the Hudson River Boom Association handled as many as twenty different drives. The river was choked.

A portion of this volume deals pictorially with logging days of old.

They were some days indeed, days when loggers worked for the magnificent sum of ninety cents a day, when a lumberjack got up at 3 a.m., ate an enormous breakfast and worked until dark. There were days when he worked until exhaustion set in, when he dried his clothes in front of a hot stove, then slept in them.

In 1880 sawmills produced the astonishing total of 325,690,000 board feet of lumber. Even before this, in 1850, New York ranked first among all states, with more than one-and-one-half billion board feet, or one-fifth the total lumber cut in the entire United States!

In 1898, more than two-thirds of the Adirondacks had been logged for softwoods; the white pine and spruce were the most unfortunate of victims. When

Virgin timber does exist in the North Country, trees either overlooked by early lumber companies, or uncut on privately held lands. This white pine still stands in a small tract of virgin timber in the northwestern Adirondacks. It could be called a survivor.

1900 began loggers were taking out 17,000,000 board feet of hardwoods. In 1933, 27,000,000 board feet were removed.

Logs were cut into thirteen-foot lengths. Pulp was cut into four-foot sections. The first pulp mill in New York was established on the Hudson River at Palmer's Falls in 1866 and by 1890 the state produced 69,274,000 board feet of pulpwood — all this in addition to everything else.

There are those who view the Forest Preserve and its mature growth with an eye for lumbering. Some refer to the preserve as a "decaying forest" in need of harvesting. Others would like to see the entire preserve lumbered under modern, scientific methods. Others want it left alone. Arguments continue.

From a personal standpoint there has been a high degree of satisfaction in compiling this volume. I have endeavored to treat not only the Adirondack Park but its fringes. A solid mix of stories has been sought.

Conditions in the Adirondack region, which covers one-fifth of the state's land mass, have changed mightily since the days when Joseph Bonaparte, older brother of Napoleon, contemplated creation of an empire in the northwestern section, and that story is gone into in some detail.

I have been fascinated with a small cottage atop Mt. McGregor in Saratoga County where President Grant spent his final days. The fascination rests not only with the central figure but in an Indian confidante who became a close friend and aide during the tumultous years of the Civil War. The story of Ely S. Parker is included. Remember him as you tour the cottage, now overshadowed by a prison.

Probably one of the most interesting stories in the Lake Champlain area involves a fort which no longer exists, built on quicksand. The sands didn't swallow it but its brief history will give you a chuckle. It was constructed on foreign soil!

Thousands of individuals were concerned over the brutal treatment shown horses in transport on the Northway. For the first time that story is described in detail, showing from start to finish how a trailer load of horses, stopped in the North Hudson area by State Police, changed the law of the state.

I have used pictures of yesteryear in what I consider abundance. There is reason. The Adirondacks today are wide open to the traveler. Once almost inaccessible places are now reachable by highway. No longer do stagecoaches ferry city folk from Amsterdam to Speculator or Indian Lake. No longer do they rumble along the dirt highway between Old Forge and Blue Mt. Lake; the road is paved and the automobile is supreme. There are thousands upon thousands of acres now open to the public, to hunters, hikers and campers. The High Peak region, particularly Mt. Marcy, is used so frequently that trails continue to show depressing signs of erosion. The question has come up: Should the state charge fees to climb? This, too, is open to debate. There are points to both sides.

Old times bear reviewing.

There is a chapter devoted in detail to selected wildlife. Three species are included, the moose, panther and timber wolf. These supposedly are extinct in the Adirondacks. But are they?

In keeping with the wildlife theme a separate chapter has been devoted to a story of tragedy and warmth; documented is the rough existence suffered by an American bald eagle during this, The Year of the Eagle.

If the eagle had rough going, consider the plight of a human of years gone by, the last woman hanged in Herkimer County and possibly in the country. It is a story worth retelling, involving as it does, the first indications that women were getting fed up with what they termed discriminatory practices in justice.

Two major figures in the Adirondack scene have passed away during the months previous to the writing of this volume. One is Harold K. Hochschild, founder of the Adirondack Museum at Blue Mt. Lake. The other is Ira Gray, a noted woodsman and hunter, Northville, who died in Glens Falls Hospital. Tribute has been paid both; such men are not to be forgotten simply because they have vanished physically from the scene.

The author has done much research in an effort to retain accuracy but errors do happen. If any have occurred I express regrets; qualify those regrets with the thought that historical happenings in particular are debatable in many respects because of different versions, as debatable as the Washington legend of chopping down a cherry tree — which incident, incidentally, has its supporters and detractors.

Mostly, I have tried in this volume, as in Volumes 1 and 2 of Adirondack Album, to preserve the drama and interest which the mountains have to offer in story and photo form. At the same time I have tried to maintain an easy-to-read, informal style of writing. I quarrel with no spellings. For instance, you may find two versions of the Boquet River. Up to about the middle of this writing, the name commonly used was Bouquet. Since that time efforts have been made to change it to Boquet. Either way it refers to the famous river which drops sharply at Split Rock Falls — an area now owned by the state as a result of a gift by the Richard W. Lawrence family of Elizabethtown.

For an opener to this book, your attention is called to what happens when a newspaperman turns into a diluted Tarzan in the Adirondack wilds!

Survival of The Unfittest

"Go Ye Forth With Bow And Arrow And
Survive" The Editor Told His
Pale Face Reporter, And For
A Moment In Life The Scribe
Managed To Do Just That!

See the funny man in the nice canoe. See how the funny man weighs too much and the front end of the canoe sticks way up in the air. See how the wind catches the front end of the canoe and see how the funny man glares as he paddles in circles. Where is the funny man going?

He is going upstream on an Adirondack river. And why is the man going upstream on an Adirondack river?

He is going upstream because his boss told him to. And what kind of a boss would tell a paunchy, pale, funny man to paddle a canoe up a river?

A newspaper editor is what kind of a boss. And did the man in the canoe which was turning circles in the wind manage to paddle up the river?

He did.

And what happened after that?

This story happened after that, that's what.

* * * * * *

It wasn't a set-up.

It was purely the natural result of talking too much at the wrong time. Many of us possess such a gift.

It occurred during the split of the century (current one, naturally), one night as I sat at the City Desk of The Times-Union, a seasoned newspaperman but a comparatively newcomer to the paper.

I had minimized the written accomplishments of a western outdoorsman who had taken to the wilderness of the Rockies to prove that indominatable Man, having once lived in the trees, in caves and on the ground, could once again survive as a Tarzan, armed only with primitive tools. My comment was that the feat didn't amount to much.

Unfortunately it was overheard by the late George Williams, a helis-on-fire-let's-put-it-out editor who stood some 40 feet distant. His hearing was acute. He could pick up the stomp of an angry chipmunk's foot on foam rubber at 100 yards.

"So," saith he, "you think anybody can do it?"

"Not anybody, but a heck of a lot of us could," I replied.

I sensed trouble when a crafty look replaced the questioning one.

"How about you?" he asked.

"Me?"

"You," came the quick answer, "and that's an order. Go forth and survive!"

He turned to leave.

"Just a cotton-pickin' moment!" I yelped. "If this is a Tarzan kind of thing, who's the Jane going along?"

"No Jane," was the answer. "Keep yourself company. Get a chimp."

I remember the scene well. Bill Lowenberg of Delmar, a colleague, was also at the desk. So was the late Hal Kallenburg, who was looking amused. Williams, I reflected morosely, had a great sense of humor. Under certain conditions he was a man to avoid.

Adventures, both great and small, start in such unusual fashion. I don't know exactly how to designate this one, but that's why I found myself two days later entering my heap and driving off, after first depositing thereon one canoe and therein one long bow, a quiver of arrows with target points and broadheads, and one hunting knife.

Also in my possession was one reflex camera with a self timer and a few rolls of film. A self timer is a blessed event on a camera; it allows a delayed exposure and thus one can take photos of one's self. The entire list, however, was not a prepossessing one for a Safari of Survival, since the stipulation was that I would start the trip minus food and matches. In other words, I was to live off the land.

My destination was the Oswegatchie River in the Northwestern Adirondacks, a scene which I had previously visited and have visited since. It would be impossible to literally get lost, since to anyone possessing reasonable logic, the return route would be downstream, provided, of course, the original portion of the trip was upstream. I noted this interesting fact in my logbook.

I aimed at launching the craft in the river at a spot called Inlet, which is not to be confused with the Inlet which is southwest of Raquette Lake, where folks today hold such uproarious events as an annual Black Fly Derby to see who can be bitten the least after proper and decent exposure.

A one-lane dirt road, remarkably free of turn-offs in event one met another car or a broad-beamed cottontail, led to the launch site from the Star Lake area. It was upstream from the man-made lake called Cranberry, which was enlarged to its present size in 1867 after construction of a log-crib dam on the Oswegatchie; said dam was authorized by the New York State Legislature.

This river which flows north, rises south of Cranberry, with waters feeding from Gull and Partlow Lakes, along with other small tributaries. The area was heavily lumbered in years long gone; once was the refuge of panthers and timber wolves desperately trying to avoid bounty hunters — described in Volume One of Adirondack Album.

The lake itself proved an atrocity of planning when the dam was put in, because land was not cleared and backed up waters not only enlarged the existing lake but moved inexorably into lakeside valleys, flooding standing timber, killing it, creating ghastly ghosts and horrendous handicaps to boaters.

It might not be remiss to point out that once upon a time, possibly up to around 1940 or so, that Cranberry Lake was a noted brook trout fishery, but misfortune arrived when "bait fish" were dumped into the basin. The brookie population went down, and bass and perch took over.

Now, because of acid rain, the bass and perch are diminishing but reportedly the brook trout are on the increase! As of this writing, they seem to be "doing well" despite acidity and it is believed they will continue to do so for the next several years if present conditions remain. Brook trout are stocked in the tributaries, including the upper stretches of the Oswegatchie, by air. The river is yet to be monitored on rise or fall of trout population.

It might also be wise to point out the section of the river being discussed is now closed to motor travel; it is wilderness area — which is also the reason trout are stocked by air, not truck. The launch site mentioned is still in use but is state-owned and has room for about twenty-four cars. The access road from Rt. 3 is now gravel; entry continues to be made in the Star Lake area.

There is legend to the origin of the river's name. One tale has it that Indian loggers were hauling logs with a team of horses on the frozen river surface when the ice gave way and the horses fell into a pool. Suitable exer-

tions led the frightened animals to safe ground, to the cries of "Hoss we gotcha" and the phrase, oft repeated, rapidly developed into Oswegatchie. True? Who knows?

In topographical aspect, the region is not exactly High Peaks in appearance; this part of the Adirondacks hasn't as yet been lifted by subterranean hell's fires and massive forces as has the former. The river is a channel which has more twists and turns than a belly dancer practicing her abdominal arts in a black fly housing development.

The water appears rust-reddish but is clear; in areas it coils silently and somberly through one of the most desolate of North Country regions. At normal height it is shallow in some spots, deeper in others where pools have formed. There were times when I felt the world's greatest collection of boulders rested therein. I managed to scrape at least 80 percent. The reason for this was simple:

At whim, Mother Nature, who can turn into a Ma Barker of gangster era fame, creates a brisk breeze and the wind will veer the bow of a canoe at right angles to the course desired. All this because the weight is in the stern and the bow is out of water. Eventually I had to beach the craft and load the front with rocks for stabilization. It worked.

This region, once seared by what is considered the greatest forest fire in the North Country in 1908, also felt the terrific impact of the Nov. 25, 1950 hurricane winds which swept Northern New York, and fallen trees still rested like flattened cornstalks, some literally uprooted, many of them giant white pines; some splintered at the base, all forming a dense, almost inpenetrable mass which would have defied a slimmed-out weasel on a weight-watching diet. Such was the fury of the battering ram which Nature decreed in that strange year.

As not so casually mentioned, I began this one-man trek to immortality without matches and an equal amount of food. That was the arrangement made with Editor Williams back in Albany; my person and canoe had been searched at port of entry by a male member of the Sevey family. I might add that Mr. Sevey, who ran a canoe rental at the site (now owned by the state), was a man who knew the river intimately. He, however, used a small outboard (then legal) with the lower half of a pitch fork lashed to the motor's stem, an ingenious arrangement since as the propeller approached an inevitable rock, the curved tines would collide first, lifting the motor until the barrier had been cleared. Mr. Sevey, viewing me with some degree of pity, offered food, but I explained I had eaten at Tupper Lake.

Thus imbued with the proper proteins, I began the trip to prove that a reputedly civilized Lord Fauntleroy could maintain comfort by existing as a somewhat bemused Neanderthal — all for the sake of an impatient editor then existing in total civilized comfort about 160 miles distant. I canoed with what I now consider moronic abandon through an October thunder, lightning and hail storm and winced as hail, the size of marbles, bounced off my noggin. If one seeks the wild life, one

Nature moves in inexorable fashion. The Oswegatchie is a comparatively mild-mannered stream, but wickedly erosive. These skeletal white pines have toppled either because of the water's bite or the hurricane which swept the area. Upper tree sections have been cut away by Forest Rangers.

does not travel under a roof. I was most assuredly not a Cleopatra skimming the Nile.

One cannot pursue the course I did without observing the large number of enjoyments Nature offers.

Some trees had been blown into and across the narrow river. Progress, therefore, was slow, but, then, I reflected, so was Napoleon's when he moved on Moscow. The difference here was that Napoleon could retreat at will. I couldn't; Napoleon didn't have George Williams as an editor.

If trees formed barriers, so did beaver dams; I recall bulling the canoe laboriously over and around breaks in the rodents' dams at least ten times before accommodating my muscles and ending the day.

Later I found that the best thing about a porcupine is that while it may taste like warmed-over dog, this obtuse animal, also a member of the rodent family, offers gracious responsibility to the consumer. It furnishes its own toothpicks.

I was not alone on the river. On one occasion I spotted a merganser on a rock; this diving, fish-eating duck is sometimes known as a "goosander," and don't ask me why. It seemed to be an amiable creature until it spotted a fish, at which time there was a flurry of violence and the squirming quarry involuntarily left its

natural environment. I thereupon cogitated upon the inequalities offered by Nature. Here was a bird with an I.Q. of probably zero, catching fish with what I considered its nose. And here was an adult male, I.Q. unknown, unable to duplicate the feat. A similar distinction came to mind when I observed a woodpecker, already fat, busily knocking holes in a dead tree to seek bugs.

By this time, I had entered the water a number of times to bull the canoe, and had wet feet. Once again the inequality of status: The beaver had inner fur which was water repellant. I had pacs which were not when immersed above their flood line.

Then, too, there was the question of eating. Everything which moved seemed to be enjoying some kind of a menu, whether it was deer which I frightened in swampy areas, or an occasional beaver interrupted in consuming bark and twigs. Such scenes evoked the deepest of all envies.

Several miles upstream I finally arrived at my destination, the leanto at Griffin Rapids. The name is misleading; there was indeed a swirl or two, but they were juvenile and hardly could be compared to the Upper Hudson. Beaching the canoe was a simple matter; inspecting the leanto proved equally simple and offered relief from aching muscles.

Left: The "survivor" creates fire with bow and spindle. Note slight evidence of smoke at base. Right: Blowing tinder in which a spark has been created into flame. Success!

Not recommended unless you grow fur and have a flat tail: The author reasoned if beaver can eat wood, there must be something to it. There isn't, even if dunked in water.

I had passed no one, coming or going, and the leanto was empty save for limp boughs on the floor, soon replaced with balsam, white pine and ferns, not the best, but still a mattress.

The next step was to create fire, not too difficult a job, since during my Boy Scout days I had mastered the bow and spindle method. There is no magic to this. A bowstring of leather (one of my pac laces) was wrapped once around the spindle; the spindle is held forcefully against a base of notched wood, and by pulling the small bow back and forth, the spindle revolves and friction creates first smoke, then a spark in tinder placed in the notch. Simple; it takes only about 20 minutes when one is in a hurry and is an excellent way to stop smoking, particularly when only dry wood can be used.

You blow the spark into a flame and gradually build a conflagration suitable to your needs. For tinder I used a stringy substance I found stuffed between the logs of the leanto. Cedar bark, shredded, will do the same thing.

Fire thus proved no problem, and once that was solved, an atmosphere of cheer prevailed. Warmth does that. So does a healthy, controlled blaze. Note in logbook: "What would Man do without fire?" Answer: "Freeze."

If fire proved no problem, working up a menu did, and this is where I met Henrietta.

Photographed during the "survival" jaunt, this picture shows a small section of a beaver dam — one of many — opened by humans to allow boat passage. The industrious rodents, however, are prepared for such disasters, usually repair the damage within a few days. The conflict is a never-ending battle.

A sizeable growth of tree upon which a beaver has started its work. The tree runs about nine or ten inches in diameter, poses no great problem for the animals, who never need dentures. Their cutters continue growing.

Henrietta is, or was, a partridge in good health — that is, she remained in good health up to the point where an arrow sent her soul soaring heavenward and left her body behind. It was, I must admit, a lucky shot; she must have been meditating as she perched on a low limb. I can truthfully say that while I have never released the brakes on any baby carriage parked on a hill, or fed poison to any pigeon who awakens me at an ungodly hour with its nonsensical coos, I had no compunction whatsoever in commiting acupuncture on the lady.

She represented food and my stomach at this point had a "to-let" sign out and needed occupancy. Of course I could have fought the field mice in the leanto for scattered crumbs left by previous occupants but even though deep in the wilderness, with only God to observe, I felt it would constitute a loss in dignity, and that was about all I possessed. Furthermore, the mice got to the crumbs first and as I was taught in my youth, possession is nine points of the eating.

Henrietta's few ounces, spitted over flames, proved most satisfactory. I could not help but feel how lucky I was compared, let us say, to those I had left behind. Here was I, seated in darkness, bedeviled by no electric lights, no telephones to answer, no living room Cyclopean Eye to devour my attention, gnawing the bones of a new-found friend departed only recently from this

While not of great height, High Falls on the Upper Oswegatchie River offers a refreshing stop for the hiker or canoeist. This upstream flow is an impassable barrier to any brook trout and in years past the area proved a productive fishing ground for the brookies. The photo was taken by the author on a "non-survival" trip! Today the trout fishery has diminished.

world, unseasoned, burned in portions to a crisp, while those unfortunate to be back in Albany were enduring unimaginable misery at a table laden only with steaks, potatoes, vegetables; possibly even going through the additional misery of being forced to eat lobster or king crab dipped in butter; all this being topped off (or preceded by) a cup of hot coffee or a cocktail or after-dinner liqueur, while I, happy adventurer, could sip spring water on-the-rocks, literally.

The feeling of sorrow was only temporary, however, since I bedded down and slept throughout the night, awakening only at intervals to 1/ bang my fist on the leanto's side to scatter curious mice, 2/ let out a yell to let deer passing nearby on their way to the river know I was present, and 3/ to replenish the fire, which had the appetite of a starved wolf.

I think the rest of the trip as less than climactic; I had one meal, and that amounted to a few ounces of seared porcupine. This girdler of trees was shot out of a tree and the principal job was of skinning, which I managed without being punctured unduly. I did think, in performing this surgery, that there were those roaming the woods far more capable than I, since the porky, or woods-pig as it is sometimes called, falls prey to the wolf, the bear or the fisher, a member of the weasel

family. I have never seen the battle which must occur before the porcupine relinquishes life and happiness, but it must be horrific, since the weapon of an attacker is the mouth with its teeth, a susceptible area for injury, or the paw used as a lever. I have seen pelts of the fisher, sometimes called the "black cat" or pekan, the undersides of which contained scores of the barbed quills; obviously the spines had worked their way into the areas without harming the consuming animals. But I still find it difficult to understand how or why the porcupine is deliberately sought as a food source, even, I might add, by a wandering newspaperman.

Not too far upstream from Griffin Rapids is High Falls, where the Oswegatchie takes a dip of beauty and force. Even here the lumberjack of long ago went after the white pines, and one of the stories still told today concerns a company which cut some of the standing virgins "by mistake." The stand was supposed to remain. But, then, many similar "mistakes" were made in those days of grab and cut.

High Falls constituted the end of the journey or, at least, half of it. I figured if I had traveled ten miles upstream, it would be the same downstream or, as I preferred to call it, "downhill." Another evidence I had scored high in mathematics in my schooling days.

Rest area. One of many quiet spots on the river where the canoeist can beach his craft. This photo snapped on a previous trip and obviously was taken during the black fly season — note protective head-neck covering worn by the figure. Note also flat character of the land. Below: The leanto at Griffin Rapids.

Highway system of beaver can be unique; can consist of canals such as above. Such provide routes into feeding areas and, on occasion, escape channels from carnivores.

So the canoe's bow was pointed north and the air was crisp and clean and the woodland smells pleasant, save in swampy areas, where gas bubbles rose from rotting masses beneath and popped forth odors comparable to an egg left unattended too long.

Admittedly I was hungry, needed a shave and a hot bath; I had added no poundage, but I had created a memory, never to go out of mind.

And, too, I had created a story, perhaps one of trivial importance, but one once written I still preserve on newsprint now turning brown and fragile.

I found that Man indeed can live in a primitive situation, but he needed the tools. For a brief time he existed in the era of one of the first guided missiles — the arrow.

I also found that Mr. Williams, who had sent me on this wild "goosander" chase, could be pleased as well. He ran the resulting story full page.

My gratitude was expressed in a tangible way.

He almost wept with joy when I presented him not with an apple, but with a fistful of porcupine quills and a small bag of Henrietta's feathers.

Two strikes and finally a home run. It is not unusual to find instances where beaver have been interrupted in their work of gnawing. Photo shows a tree which has been attacked three times. A predator could have interfered the first time or two, or perhaps inclement weather such as storms.

The Little Fort That Wouldn't Stand Still

**A Decision, Born of Fear, Resulted
in Considerable Embarrassment
to America's National Dignity**

When an international border turns into a rubber band, something has to give.

In this case, it was not only national dignity, but a United States fort which, once it was partially built, became a victim of confused identity and created loud howls of derisive laughter in the North Country.

The United States Army constructed the outpost on its northern frontier at Rouses Point in northern New York, but Canada was able to claim it. The reason was simple and valid at the time. It was constructed on Canadian soil!

This, then, is the story of a stone and brick fort, built on quicksand, which became famous internationally as Fort Blunder. It is known by no other name.

It is also the story of its successor, Fort Montgomery, also located at Rouses Point on the shore of Lake Champlain.

Fort Blunder is memory; there is no physical evidence of consequence which exists.

Fort Montgomery remains skeletal. It has been figuratively bombed out by the bite of time, the elements, and the fact that much of its stone was used in the 1930's to build a bridge linking New York State and Vermont.

Fort Blunder, of course, makes the better story.

Its origin was based upon the fact that England never quite got over nursing the headaches of losing the American Revolution. Britain, still a powerful nation unwilling to admit it had lost a major war, still considered America easy plucking, and for a long period harassed this country's shipping, often impressing American seamen into the Royal Navy.

The United States took it on the chin until 1812. On June 18 of that year, war was declared and soon it began to seem that British campaigns of the Revolution, still vivid in some memories, would be resurrected. America was invaded from Canada.

The war's final action was the sea capture by Americans of the British war sloop, Penguin, March 23, 1815.

But meanwhile, Britain had tried an invasion under Gen. George Provost, who rumbled down from Montreal with 12,000 men, planning on using, once again, the Old Warpath of Nations, Lake Champlain and Lake George, then moving southward into the Hudson Valley — a gesture made years earlier by Gen. "Gentleman Johnny"

At water's edge.

Burgoyne, with disastrous results at the Battle of Saratoga in 1777. Interesting to note is that Burgoyne, humiliated at this pivotal battle, never lived to follow the progress of Provost; he died in 1792. One wonders what he would have thought.

Provost was stopped at Plattsburgh for good and sufficient reason. On Sept. 11, 1814, a British naval squadron, acting in support of his legions, was defeated by American Commodore Thomas Macdonough in a clash on Lake Champlain. When Gen. Provost learned of this disconcerting news, he abandoned his land attack on Plattsburgh, abandoned the idea of becoming the conqueror of Hudson's Valley, and wisely retreated into the sanctuary of Canada.

This, and other photos of Fort Montgomery, were taken during the 1960's by John La Duke of Saranac Lake. Above is the cavernous interior, showing intricate brick work done by masons during the fort's construction.

Eventually Britain figured it had had enough on all fronts. With the war over, American military men, bitten twice by the British bug of colonial ambition, decided that fortifications along the Canadian border might serve as deterrents, just in case the British lion succumbed once again to the itch to leap the fence into greener financial pastures.

Lake Champlain's massive volume flows into the St. Lawrence River through the Richelieu River. Had this region been fortified, for instance, during the Revolution, there is the possibility that the Battle of Valcour Island, in which American ships held back the British fleet, might never have occurred. Had the same area been protected by cannon before the War of 1812, the probability is that no British vessel could have entered the lake. The outlet area is narrow enough to allow the big guns to protect it.

All this might have been revolving in the minds of military engineers as they contemplated erecting a protective barrier at Rouses Point. The site selected was at Island Point, a "small island" of sand between Rouses Point and Province Point.

It is reported that Island Point became an island only when high water hiked Champlain's level. Regardless whether it was a true island, or worked only part time at the job, one thing was certain. It held deposits of quicksand, loose, wet sand, gifted with a gargantuan appetite for swallowing, if not digestion.

The idea of fortifying Island Point originated in 1814, but the Army found itself sufficiently busy trading blows with the English until the following year, and by the time plans had been drawn and bureaucratic processes had been completed, construction did not start until 1816.

It was not easy.

In 1816, a thoroughly unexpected, unwanted "contribution" was furnished by the massive eruption of the Tambora volcano in Indonesia, the world's largest archipelago, which lies along the equator SE of Asia and N and NW of Australia. This explosion of thunder, lava and dust created an enormous cloud of volcanic debris which floated at great height not only over Western Europe but America's Northeast, shutting off or filtering sunlight and its warmth in the Blunder Area.

Temperatures dropped as the vast shroud hovered overhead.

That year has come down through history as the famous "Year Without a Summer." Snow fell in June. And it fell in July. Ice formed on ponds. September saw early frost. Crops failed. Sheep which had been sheared, reportedly froze to death. Foresters in the late 1800's found that even tree growth was affected. In some instances, growth rate almost ceased, with thickness of rings for this year "almost microscopic" in width. The wintery conditions existed throughout the Northeast and losses suffered by many were so devastating they migrated into the Midwest.

If weather conditions were bad, the quicksand was worse. Col. Joseph Totten, later to become Chief of Engineers for the Army, had established headquarters at Rouses Point in 1816. He was capable but not happy; he faced odds which were tremendous.

The quicksand proved ever starved.

Obviously no fort worth shooting at or from can be built without a solid foundation. And to establish one, Col. Totten ordered a multitude of objects thrown into the pit, which soon gave the appearance of being bottomless. The idea of using it as a junkyard was, of course, to fill it until material thrown in reached firm earth or bedrock and thus firmness would be built from the bottom up.

Into the area went pickets, or stakes found and moved from the Old Plattsburgh battleground, a site previously occupied by the American forces facing Gen. Provost. Added to these were stumps, transported from miles around, some of them pulled from their anchor of decades. Logs of hemlock, pine, birch, beech, ash and other varieties were tossed into the sea of mud, as were piles of brush, loads of earth, stone, scrap lumber and even rails.

Eventually it was thought solid ground existed. In a way, it did. A man could walk upon it without disappearing from family and friends.

The contractors hired by the Army were three Scotchmen, all experienced stone cutters, including Malcomb McMartin, James MacIntyre and John Stewart. These sturdy gentlemen were expected to construct the 30-foot-high walls of the octagonal fort, expected to surround about three-quarters of an acre.

There was good news for makers of bricks. The estimated cost of the fort, approximately $200,000, included the purchase and installation of three million.

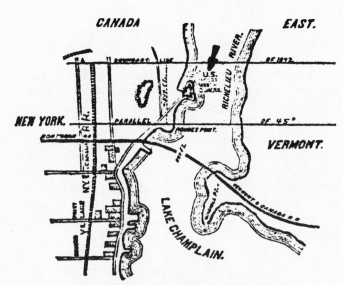

ROUSE'S POINT AND VICINITY.

Map copied from a history of Clinton and Franklin Counties. Arrow points to location of both Fort Blunder and Fort Montgomery at Lake Champlain's northern end, at Rouses Point. The military advantage is obvious; any invasion from Canada, using the Richelieu River, would receive an extraordinary "welcome" from American defenders.

Among labor battalions were infantrymen from the Sixth Regiment stationed to the south at Plattsburgh. They were ordered to the scene in June, 1818.

They arrived.

And they departed, many of them, specifically for Canada. Desertions ran at such volume that on August 15, less than three months later, they were hurriedly "recalled" to Plattsburgh where they were put to work on road construction.

The United States government then became a true equal opportunity employer. Local labor was hired.

The spirit, Col. Totten found, was strong, but the ground wasn't. The foundation walls cracked, heaved and joined the junk buried below. The earth was still ravenous. More material was thrown in.

Finally, either the bottom of the quicksand was reached, or the earth simply gave up the struggle. Foundation walls began to remain above ground, take shape. Victory seemed possible.

While this was going on, the United States and Britain, still sparring, even if diplomatically, decided they needed a positive, permanent boundary. Some historians say this was due to British insistence more than American.

The Treaty of Ghent provided for such determination. To fulfil this obligation, it was necessary for surveyors to locate and place the 45th degree of N. latitude, which line apparently had long been considered the one of demarcation. Its exact placement on the map was needed.

No one in the United States seemed particularly perturbed when the survey began in 1818, two years after the construction began.

There was, however, consternation in January, 1819, and the reason for it was explained vividly in this extract from a history of Clinton County:

"In October, 1818, the astronomical agents of Great Britain and the United States commenced the survey of the line of latitude 45 degrees north, which had been designated as the boundary line. In January, 1819, to the chagrin of our government, the fort was found to be on Canadian soil, nearly a mile north of the boundary line!

"Orders were immediately given to suspend all operations until the question of site could be definitely arranged and settled. It is said the contractors sued the government for the amount of contract and obtained full damages."

The fact that America had built a fort to protect itself from British Canada, in British Canada, created much derisive comment from Canadians and Americans alike, who promptly dubbed the unfortunate site Fort Blunder. Fort Blunder it has remained.

Gloom may have settled over the White House, then occupied by President James Monroe, to whom the site was familiar since he visited it in 1817, but the same gloom did not settle over the residents in the fort's vicinity.

There was loot to be had.

Stone and brick became "common property." So did copper and iron abandoned on the site. Homes were constructed from the stone pilfered. A school house was constructed. So was a church in Rouses Point.

The plundered Blunder became memory, its location nestled 4,576 feet within Canada.

This was the scene in 1819 and for several years afterward. However, all was not lost. Diplomacy runs a peculiar course at times. Its path may vanish into a cavern and reappear at the other end, in sunshine.

This was the case in the Fort Blunder episode. The United States was never happy with the decision that placed the boundary south of the Blunder site.

Twenty-three years later, a final decision was made. Amazingly, a provision of the Webster-Ashburton Treaty in 1842 reestablished the line; the old boundary was confirmed; Fort Blunder, or at least its location, was back in the good old U.S.A.! The rubber band had snapped back into place.

Portions of the ruins of Fort Montgomery are shown in background, forming a backdrop for two enthusiastic youngsters.

Fort Montgomery, named after the American general, Richard Montgomery, who was killed in 1775 at the futile siege of Quebec, thereupon moves into the picture.

This is the fort which today remains in skeleton form. It rests near the site of the abandoned Blunder. Friction still existed between the states and Canada; border incidents were frequent. The idea of another fort held firm.

This time, the quicksands were conquered. Huge pilings, made of logs, were driven in 1844 deep into the sands, into depths ranging from 15 to 55 feet. This time enormous steam-driven pile drivers were used. Numbered in the hundreds, pilings held firm. Over the mass of timber were placed squared off trunks of hemlock, in the form of a giant mattress; on this platform was to be built the stone work.

The area surrounding the fort and the fort itself occupied about three acres, of which the fort consumed one. Five bastions were proposed, more than had been proposed for Fort Blunder. Stone was quarried on Grand Island and cut to form there, later to be transported by boat. Some of the blocks weighed as much as ten tons.

The fort was to be garrisoned by 800 men and upon completion would command the channel opening from the Richelieu into Lake Champlain. Hundreds of men worked long and mightily upon the project.

The progress was not without interruption; work was stopped when money ran out. By the time of the Civil War, the foundation was firm and some of the east and north walls were up to their appointed height of almost 50 feet. The structure was built to accommodate 90 cannon.

When Fort Sumter was shelled on April 12, 1861, at Charleston Harbor, South Carolina, thus marking the beginning of the Civil War, President Lincoln ordered the completion of Fort Montgomery and money was appropriated. By 1862 about one third of its fire power was installed, and by 1865, the year the war ended, it had received its full armament, even though final construction stages had not been completed.

Lincoln died in the same year and Andrew Johnson assumed the presidency. Work was permanently suspended in 1870 and the post abandoned in 1908. Between 1870 and 1908 the fort was "garrisoned" by an ordnance sergeant. In 1910, armanent was removed. Thereafter, disintegration began; vandals destroyed what they could, and everything movable was taken by thieves; thus occurred the pattern of Fort Blunder once again.

The final assault on the fort was in the 1930's when stone work was removed to be used in the construction of the bridge linking Rouses Point and Alburg, Vermont.

Neither Fort Blunder nor Fort Montgomery ever fired a single shot in defense of the United States.

As far as is known, only one attempt was made by a "world power" to capture it. This occurred in 1865 when Captain Gustave A. Drolet of the 65th Canadian Volunteers borrowed a horse and buggy and drove out of Lacolle, Quebec, to look the situation over. When he reached the village of Champlain, he found himself contained in a parade, part of memorial ceremonies held on the day of President Lincoln's burial.

The captain also found himself attending services in a church. He then found himself a respected guest at a dinner, since he was considered a representative of the British government, sent to share the sorrow.

Apparently Drolet shared not the sorrow, but a goodly quantity of bourbon, because he became immobilized and when finally he sobered up, he relinquished all plans of assault and capture, and returned to his post!

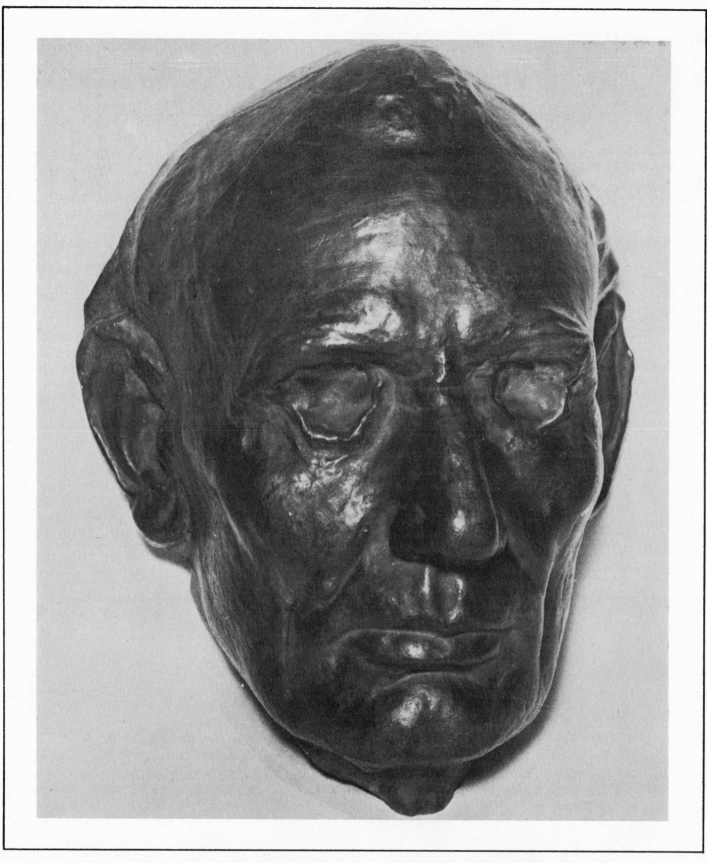

It would be safe to say that Lincoln, who authorized completion of Fort Montgomery at Rouses Point, never saw the fort nor the area even though as President he was fully aware of the overall importance of the fortification. Lincoln was assassinated in 1865, four years after he ordered the fort to full completion.

Photos of Lincon are fairly common. But the above, believed to be the death mask of the man whose burden was the Civil War, is, by comparison, little seen. The author was fortunate in being able to photograph the mask (cast into metal) while it was briefly in the Albany area some years ago.

14

The Final Days

The Man Fought Not Only Pain
But Poverty. As Death Approached
Did He, In The Solitude of
The Hills, Think Of The Seneca
Chief Who Helped Him Turn
The Tide of History?

In capsule form, a riddle: He was born the son of a farmer. In Illinois he lived in a log cabin. He was a clerk in a country store. His rise to prominence did not begin until he was 40 years of age. He saw the horrors of the Civil War at first hand. He was a man of tremendous determination and patience.

He occupied the White House.

Among his most notable achievements as President was in the political-social world, in the enactment of the 15th amendment to the Constitution of the United States, which specifies suffrage should not be restricted because of race, color or previous conditions of servitude.

* * * * * *

Abraham Lincoln?

Wrong.

Hiram Ulysses Grant?

Correct.

Call him also Ulysses Simpson Grant, 18th President of the United States; both names fit the man; he was born with the former and a congressmen's "supposition" changed it to the latter, and thus history will know him as such forever.

On the verge of poverty, he spent his last, agonizing days in the Palmertown Range of the Adirondacks, at Mt. McGregor, Town of Wilton, Saratoga County, in a modest cottage loaned by a wealthy New York City family — a building perched on a 1,300-foot-high rounded peak.

When he occupied it in 1885, a resort hotel was nearby; a steam railroad ran from Saratoga Springs northward to near the summit. Today the railroad is long gone. So is the hotel. In its place is an incongruous, grim complex, the Mt. McGregor Correctional Facility, a minimum security prison surrounded by woodlands. From the wide cottage veranda one can see the stone walls and the high wire fencing, topped with coils of barbed wire. It is not a prepossessing sight; offers disconcerting contrast to the small building below.

In this cottage Grant lived only a short six weeks. Within its quiet interior, surrounded by his family, he became an enfeebled man, his neck constantly wrapped in a scarf, beset by the constant devil of pain. It was here in the mountains where, unable to communicate save by written notes, he completed his military memoirs for publisher Mark Twain.

The manuscript was finished four days before he died of cancer of the throat. He personally never enjoyed the financial returns. His family, however, received the half million dollars in income the memoirs generated and that would have pleased the general mightily, since it was for his wife, the former Julia T. Dent, and his children, that he wrote them.

It is not where a man dies, but how.

Grant died evidencing the same raw courage he displayed throughout a life of ups and downs; the same courage that made him merciless in the expenditure of manpower during Civil War battles, and yet with the same sensitivity that made him unable to stand the sight and sounds of surgeons at work on the battle wounded.

He was a man of contradictions. He was a man so closely tied in affection and respect with a Seneca Indian chief that he made that sachem his confidential aide in Civil War years and during his presidential years, his Commissioner of Indian Affairs.

It is possible that the Seneca's friendship prompted to a great extent the 15th U.S. Constitutional amendment already mentioned. Even after attaining political heights, a man's personal emotions serve as guides.

The Seneca was Ha-sa-no-an-da, known as Ely S. Parker to the whites. He was born near Indian Falls, Genesee County, in 1828. He graduated from Rensselaer Polytechnic Institute, Troy, N.Y., as a civil engineer and his ability was soon recognized. He became superintendent of improvements at the western end of the Erie Canal.

Parker found his man in Grant, as later developments proved, and it makes an intensely interesting story, even

Above photo, a copy of another, shows Grant in beaver hat and wearing his usual scarf, as he sat on the veranda writing his memoirs.

He resigned his commission in 1854, turned to farming and real estate and did not succeed well in either field; he then moved to Galena, Illinois, where he clerked for an annual salary of $800 in his father's leather goods store.

Here the careers of Grant and Parker joined in most unusual fashion.

The story goes that when Grant got drunk in those days, he got into trouble. In this instance, it was a fight outside a Galena saloon. Grant, a man who stood at five-feet, eight-inches, was getting pummeled heavily when a giant of a man entered the fray, grabbed Grant's opponent by the scruff of the neck and the seat of his pants, and heaved him into the dust of the street.

The giant was Ely Parker. The reason he was in Galena was a business one; he was supervising construction of a customs house and marine hospital in that community.

Grant and Parker became friends; Parker the listener, Grant the dreamer, the man on the verge of world-wide fame, who never suspected in the least the part he would play in the approaching chaos.

The meeting could be termed a gesture of Fate. The two were to come together again, later, at a time when both were in need of the other.

though there is a curious contradiction evident to the visitor at Grant's Cottage. While many photographs and paintings adorn the walls, there is no photograph of Parker, even though the two were bound by friendship and war for many years.

The men, however, were not to come together until Grant's years as a clerk during the 1850's. It is difficult to write of Grant without prominent mention of Parker. Their stories mesh, as will be seen.

Ulysses S. Grant was born in Point Pleasant, Ohio, April 27, 1822, and spent his early years helping his mother and father run a farm. The sunrise-to-sunset pattern did not appeal, however, even though Grant, through his love for horses, became an expert rider.

In 1839, he was appointed to West Point and it was at this academy his name underwent change. The congressman who sponsored him knew Grant by the name most called him, Ulysses. He assumed, therefore, it was his first name and for some reason added the name of his mother's family, Simpson. The transition from Hiram Ulysses to Ulysses Simpson thus became actuality.

He was not the best of students. In a class of 39 he managed to graduate 21st. And then he went to war, in Mexico. Later he was assigned to stations in California and Oregon, and it was at this time his career began to suffer from what politely might be called excessive indulgence in strong liquor.

Parker was appointed Assistant-General with rank of captain on June, 1863. He became a Brigadier-General, U.S. Army, March 2, 1867. He is shown as he held the latter rank.

16

Parker continued his work as an engineer. The Civil War was yet to come. Grant continued his pattern of life and as a friend remarked: "At this stage, he was a broken and disappointed man."

History, however, has shown that events can touch upon the human mind and body with impressive impact.

In 1861 there came the call to arms. Grant responded. He became a colonel in the 21st Illinois Regiment, then moved upward to Brigadier-General. His skills became noticeable. He was promoted to Major-General in the U.S. Volunteers.

His path, however, was not a smooth one. And, no doubt, his imbibing had something to do about strewing rocks in it. There were quarrels within the military hierarchy, and others moved around and over Grant.

But there was one man who was not only in command of, but saw the overall picture; who saw, in Grant, the leader he desired. That man was Lincoln. When Grant forced the surrender of Vicksburg on July 4, 1863, with its 30,000 troops, Lincoln made him a Major-General in the regular army.

The decision was not made without considerable disapproval based on internal jealousies. Much was made of Grant's reported drinking. And it was at this time the story came into being that Lincoln reportedly said to anti-Grant forces that if he knew the brand of whiskey Grant was taking aboard, he would send him barrels of it.

What Lincoln actually said was that if he knew the general's brand, he'd buy some for other generals who were accomplishing far less!

Whatever Grant's difficulties, he did manage to win battles. He could be accused of exorbitant expenditures of manpower, but history also can overlook this by the victories scored. The pattern was the same: Wearing down the South by constant pressure. It worked. Appomattox was the result. Who was there to quarrel with success in the bloodiest of all wars?

Illness was far from Grant's mind as the war ended. So were the Adirondack Mountains, the bulk of which was still primitive wilderness, just beginning to wince under the sharp touch of the axe and saw.

If illness was far from the man's mind, so was poverty. He still had a sense of balance and fairness, evidencing it, for instance, by saving General Robert E. Lee and fellow Southern military leaders from charges of treason, by threatening to resign if those charges were preferred.

He ran for President on the Republican ticket. He won. He ran again. He was reelected. After the Presidency, he toured the world with his wife and a son. He was welcomed throughout as a hero, which he was indeed. But a financial pit was about to open. In partnership with a man named Ward, he opened an investment firm. It collapsed. The general was left holding the bag; he was wiped out. At this point, Mark Twain stepped into the picture.

Twain may have been a humorist, but he was also a businessman. He ran his own publishing firm. He thought Grant's memoirs would sell. He inspired the general toward that effort and Grant, determined to regain security for himself and family, began to work day and night. It was not an easy task; the job of a writer is a lonely one, and the prodding must come from within.

It was about this time, 1884, he received his second devastating blow. He found he was suffering from cancer.

In the spring of 1885, Congress made him a general on the retired list. In the summer of that year, he went to Mt. McGregor, where he took up residence for six weeks in the cottage owned by the Drexel family of New York City. They were long, dreadful weeks.

His condition prevented him from sleeping in normal fashion. Leather chairs, still visible to the visitor today, were moved together, facing each other. Grant sat in one, resting his feet on the second. A small board across arm rests served as a writing table. A pencil and paper were his tools. If the chairs still exist, so does a large bottle of "sedative waters" which Grant used to rub on his tortured throat for relief. He did not encourage visitors. He explained simply by note that he was not the "best of company."

It is most difficult to imagine this famous figure, moving slowly about the residence, pulling his shawl about his shoulders, putting on his beaver hat, then sitting in his favorite chair on the veranda. It is difficult to imagine use of sanitary facilities within the room in which he wrote — a large chamber pot, conveniently placed.

Up to midnight there were electric lights in the building. The power was furnished by the Hotel Balmoral, just above the cottage. After midnight there were none, because the daily custom was to shut down the generator at the witching hour.

It was then the disabled old soldier would trim the kerosene lamp wick, light it, and continue working through the quiet hours of the early morning. The lamp remains a priceless relic. So does the candle in its holder, which source was used on occasion. Nearby is a small bureau containing articles of clothing, including a robe and shirts.

Four days before his death on July 23, 1885, he put down his pencil. His memoirs were complete. He had won his race. He took to his bed, still at the cottage. He passed away at 8:08 a.m., and the clock on the fireplace mantle was stopped by his son, Col. Fred Grant.

The air of tragedy still hangs heavily at the death scene. Had the soldier lived today, he might have been cured.

If the chairs, the bed, the clock, the furniture, and other mementos of the man remain, also in evidence for the visitor of today is a small spot atop Mt. McGregor called the "Lookout." Here Grant could sit to enjoy the mountain air and scenery; here he could see the rise of the Adirondack ranges to the north. Less than 20 miles distant was the Fort William Henry Hotel at Lake George, where he had frequently in the past lent his

Where Grant rested, wrote and slept: These two leather chairs, facing each other, were in use daily; the Civil War general sat in one, rested his feet on the other. He used a board resting on the chair's arms as a writing table. The table contains his kerosene lamp, scissors, a candle in a holder and a glass. Beneath, are a bowl and the Japanese fan Grant used on a warm day.

presence to social functions, even while Gen. William Tecumseh Sherman told Civil War stories to boggle-eyed hotel guests.

Here, too, Grant could sit and recall memories, many of them of his Seneca friend and aide, Ely Parker.

And what of him?

As stated, it is strange there is no picture of Parker visible to the visitor. Over the deathbed is a portrait of Lincoln. Other portraits adorn the walls. One room contains enormous wreaths of flowers, now dried into dusty tan, delivered upon his death. But no picture of Parker.

Which is an omission without answer. Could a friend or a member of the family have removed it?

The lives of Parker and Grant crossed for a long and endurable period. Without Grant, Parker never would have reached the heights he attained. Without Parker, the course of the Civil War might have been changed, because Parker's Indian skills and strength once saved the general from capture by a Confederate patrol. Had

such occurred, the entire history of the United States might have changed.

So Parker's story, therefore, can be another chapter to Grant's life. His story could parallel the general's in the light of difficulties experienced. Parker is considered by many as the last Grand Sachem of the Iroquois Confederacy, a man who became well known in the social circles of not only Washington but Albany.

Grant never forgot the fight he was losing outside the saloon in Galena and the fact he was saved from a vicious beating.

In a way, it is Parker's story which may have the greater inspirational value, particularly today, for his rise to greatness was accomplished in the face of the discrimination of the white man against the Indian. The day had not yet passed when the white man killed the Indian for sport in the West, or robbed him of his women for western frontier brothels.

General William Tecumseh Sherman, above, famous for his "March to the Sea" campaign, proved a close friend of Grant's.

The Revolution was over when Parker was born, but there were those who remembered that many of the Iroquois had fought side-by-side with the British; that the Seneca nation's land had been ravaged by Gen. Sullivan who, joined by Clinton's forces at Schenectady, moved like a scythe through Seneca cornfields and orchards, and that it was only after this heavy blow that many Senecas fought with, not against the revolutionaries.

It could be said, in a way, that the Iroquois back was broken by the Revolution and the usual results of defeat were evidenced for years ensuing, poverty, discrimination, broken treaties, harassment. The once great Confederacy which controlled a good share of the Northeastern United States fell upon harsh times; members were not considered citizens of the lands they occupied before whites took over. They were not slaves, as were the blacks, but almost as badly off; they had no master save a government operating with little mercy.

An overall view of the Grant Cottage, taken some years ago. The photo is believed to be by the late John Vrooman of Schenectady, widely known as a writer of historical novels and documentary volumes. It shows the veranda upon which Grant and his family often sat to enjoy the mountain air. Nearby was the Hotel Balmoral, the generator for which also fed lights in the cottage – up to midnight.

Into this dispirited atmosphere Parker was born, the son of Jo-no-es-sto-wa, Dragon Fly, or William Parker, a Seneca chief. In lineal descent he could trace his ancestry into prehistory. In his youth he saw the transition of the Indian home from bark to logs; of Indian dress from buckskin to cloth. He also felt poverty and eventually hired out as a mule driver for the British military in Canada.

It was on a mule drive to Hamilton, Ontario, that Parker received the incentive to become great. Tormented by British officers, he quit the drive in disgust, walked 100 miles to his home and school. In that moment, he realized a hard fact of life for the Indian of the day. His ancestral mode of living was gone forever. To exist, he must conform to the white man's way.

Gifted with phenomenal strength, a giant physique and a brain bordering on genius, Parker entered Yates Academy, then Cayuga Academy at Aurora, N.Y., where he first met Lewis H. Morgan, who later graduated from Union College, Schenectady, and became an authority on Iroquoian history. Morgan, like Grant, helped Parker make his climb.

After Cayuga, Parker became a student attorney in the law firm of Angel and Rice, Ellicottville, Cattaraugus County. He spent three hard years in learning the law and then met with one of the many bitter episodes in his life.

A Supreme Court decision said he could not become a lawyer. Only the white male had this "privilege!" For the first time Parker completely lost his temper and cursed — not in the language of the Senecas which contained no oaths — but in the white man's language, which did, and does.

He was, however, unbelievably resilient.

He entered RPI and, as mentioned, became a civil engineer who worked on the Erie Canal. Fellow workers remembered him as "The Indian" who recognized their identity by their footsteps, who seldom turned his head in talk as he continued on with his own work. He became resident engineer at Rochester and at the same time kept a farm, raised colts (his passion) and looked after his parents.

In 1855, as war clouds were forming, he accepted a position as chief engineer for the Chesapeake and Abermarle Canal. He surveyed the canal, drafted plans and chose the final location. He then became construction engineer for the Lighthouse District, involving Lakes Huron, Michigan and Superior. Since this was a military position, he was given the rank of Major.

Thus he moved nearer to Grant.

In 1857 while working in the Galena area, he interfered in he saloon fight already mentioned. Yet there still would remain an interval before he and Grant became close.

Parker became a Mason; was elected Grand Orator of the Grand Lodge of Illinois. The white world, he found, accepted him in that state, admired him, if he lived his own life without pretense. Thus many of his talks, (he was a powerful speaker), dealt with his position as an Indian.

Before one Masonic group he declared:

"Where shall I go when the last of my race shall have gone forever? I said 'I shall knock on the door of Masonry and see if the white race will recognize me as they did my ancestors when we were strong and the whiteman weak.' "

Gen. Ely S. Parker at the time of his marriage.

Minnie Sackett of Washington, D.C., at the time of her marriage to Gen. Parker.

Copies of daguerreotypes of Gen. Parker's mother, Elizabeth, and father, William.

In travels to the East, he found the whites did recognize him, but there were a few unfortunates who did not. In an Albany hotel, for instance, a drunk attacked him and he had to bear-hug his assailant into submission. A store owner once ordered him out of his place of business; he picked the man up and swung him in circles. The two later became friends.

But discrimination continued on occasion.

He became interested in joining the Union forces while working on levees along the Mississippi and came to Albany to tender his services to the governor of New York State. But that worthy said he wanted nothing to do with an Indian and suggested that Parker go home.

At this time, Grant was busy recruiting his Illinois regiment.

Parker persisted. He resigned his engineering job in 1862, went to Washington and offered his services to U.S. Secretary of State William H. Seward. That former New York Governor was not enthusiastic, and he told Parker:

"This is not an Indian's war. This is a white man's fight. We will settle our differences without Indian aid."

Another blow for Parker, who knew that fellow Senecas were already in uniform, and so were blacks. He returned to his farm.

And it was then, in some quiet way, that Grant moved.

Parker was literally summoned from his plow by special messenger, made Captain on the spot, and his commission was signed by Lincoln himself!

He joined Grant at Vicksburg; served by his side at Chattanooga, Lookout Mountain and Missionary Ridge. He came down with malaria and tried the usual army remedy, whiskey and quinine, but he almost instantly became a teetotaler the rest of his life for a simple reason: Whiskey made him do strange things, like chasing superior officers!

As Grant moved upward in his career, he kept Parker nearby. Their friendship grew deeper and Parker served with distinction throughout the Wilderness Campaign. His Indian skills proved of utmost value. In one instance, a Confederate patrol had moved to within 40 yards of the Grant party, and it was Parker who literally sensed its nearness. Later a Confederate captain was captured and confirmed the fact that had the Grant group moved another few yards, it would have fallen into ambush. One can imagine the consternation of the Union forces, the exuberance of the South had Grant, the supreme commander, been taken prisoner and exhibited.

On August 30, 1864, Parker became military secretary and confidante to Grant. The Seneca Sachem literally became his right hand man; proved to be more than a secretary; often served as personal bodyguard, stationing himself outside Grant's tent at night with drawn pistol.

In a way, his relationship with Grant culminated in drama at Appomattox, at Lee's surrender, for it was Parker who wrote out the original draft of surrender, a draft which he kept until his death.

Throughout the war he was known mostly as "The Indian." At Appomattox, when he was formally introduced to Gen. Lee, there was a momentary hesitation on the part of Lee, who at first thought he was black. Later accounts discount this; say that Lee extended his hand and said to Parker:

"I am proud to meet a real American." To which Parker is supposed to have answered: "General, we are all Americans."

The Seneca chief followed Grant to Washington, there was given the rank of Brigadier-General of the U.S. Volunteers and it was back-dated April 9, 1865, the day of the surrender. It was on April 26, 1869, he resigned from the War Department.

Much went on between 1865 and his resignation. He helped the Tonawanda Senecas hold onto lands which they had managed to save. He fought their battles in the halls of the New York State Legislature and in Washington.

He married Minnie Sackett of Washington, but the marriage had its unusual aspects. Originally set for Dec. 17, 1867, Parker failed to appear at the church. It was found he had been drugged by a rival suitor. At a later date, neither Parker nor Miss Sackett appeared at the church; they were married at a private ceremony to avoid incident.

A gathering of warriors, showing Grant, standing, center (brimmed hat), and Gen. Ely Parker, extreme right. The photo of Grant and Parker and staff officers was taken at Cold Harbor, Va., in May, 1864. Other officers are not identified.

During Grant's term as President, Parker was made Commissioner of Indian Affairs. He served during trying times; the department was graft-ridden and Indians were being treated as sub-humans. In the West, unscrupulous whites would sell cattle to the government, drive them to reservations, then through liquor buy them back for as little as 25 cents a head. And with the vicious killing of millions of buffalo — a deliberate blood letting by the whites to subvert the Indian by robbing him of his natural food — the plight of the Plains Indian was desperate. Parker fought for them hard; when he resigned in 1871, there was a general Indian peace.

The toll paid by the Seneca was a harsh one. His fight for decent treatment had created bitter enemies, powerful ones who forced him to appear before a Congressional committee on trumped up charges, later disproved completely. His career included the amassing of a modest fortune in New York, but he lost it because he bonded a friend who embezzled a large sum.

As an Indian, Parker was not required by law to repay the sum, but he did.

In New York he eventually became the police department architect and the department's supply clerk, a position he held until death approached. It was during this time he met such famous figures as Theodore Roosevelt and Jacob Riis, the Danish newspaper reporter.

The end was near. Grant had long gone. Parker collapsed at his desk in police headquarters and died at his Fairfield, Conn., home. His body was removed to Forest Lawn Cemetery in Buffalo in January, 1897, near the grave of another Iroquois chief, Red Jacket.

Thus Parker's life cycle was completed where it began, for it was in the area where he was buried where his tribal members came to council and to trade, and it was in this same area where Parker's mother had a vision, later explained by a medicine man in this fashion:

"A son shall be born to you who will be distinguished among his nation as a peacemaker: He will be a wise white man but will never desert his people, nor lay down his sachem's horns as a great chief. His name will reach from the East to the West, from the North to the South as great among his Indian family and pale faces. His sun will rise in Indian land and set on white man's land, yet the ancient land of his ancestors will fold him in death."

This, then, the story of Ely Samuel Parker, confidante of Grant, a Sachem of a nation that once roamed the very mountains in which the famous general died. History cannot forget them, ever.

The bed in which the enfeebled Grant died, above which hangs a picture of Lincoln, is among many items of historical value in the Grant Cottage. Members of his family were present at the time of his demise.

Among the many unusual wreaths delivered upon the general's death was this one, signifying the gates to the beyond. It was sent by the Leland Stanfords. Stanford, born in Watervliet, became a railroad builder, merchandiser, California Governor and U.S. Senator.

The card at the base reads: "This clock was stopped by Colonel Fred Grant at the moment of his father's death, 8:08 a.m., July 23, 1885." It has not been disturbed since.

One of the few photos of the Grant family gathering on the porch of the cottage in which he died. It was taken on June 19, 1885. Unfortunately, full identification is not available.

The Tragedy That Turned The Tide

In the Past the Northway Was Called "The Torture Trail" By Many. This Is the Story How Dedicated People Changed An Out-of-Date Law

Shipments of horsemeat from the United States are running about one hundred million pounds annually. Exports during 1980 alone involved well over 300,000 head. Much of the meat, prized for its high protein content, is destined for France and other European markets.

—— News item

* * * * * *

Shortly after midnight, Saturday, December 12, 1980, Troopers Ed Haroff, Bob Carlson and Paul Manning, working out of the State Police station in the village of Schroon Lake, were alerted to an incident of cruelty on the Northway, which was to shock not only New York State but to lead eventually to a change in a state law.

A gas station attendant at Pottersville, Warren County, had noted what appeared to be a dead horse in a loaded northbound trailer which had stopped briefly to gas up.

At 1:30 a.m., Trooper Carlson spotted a truckload of horses in transport to a Canadian slaughterhouse, where, once butchered, the carcasses would be processed for shipment abroad, where the appetite for horsemeat, called hippophagy, is common. Trooper Carlson halted the truck. He thereupon radioed Troopers Haroff and Manning, also on patrol, and was joined by them within minutes.

At first glance, on this snowy and lonely night, there was nothing particularly unusual about the scene; the Northway has been, and is, often used as a highway for domesticated animals destined for Canadian abattoirs and the human stomach. What proved shocking, however, was that when the trailer was inspected, Troopers Carlson, Haroff and Manning found a scene almost unbelievable.

Eighty-five horses and ponies were crammed into a trailer built to hold only 35.

They were packed back to back, side to side, head to head. Many were in an agony helpless to remedy. Smaller animals, for instance, once they lowered their heads, were unable to again raise them; thus their muzzles remained only a few inches above the floor. Excrement and urine covered the trailer floor. The stench rose in heavy, heated waves.

Five were found trampled to death. Four were found so heavily injured they were ordered destroyed on the spot by Dr. Robert A. Lopez, Westport veterinarian called by State Police, a man who also is head of the North Country Society for the Prevention of Cruelty to Animals.

The vehicle and its mutilated cargo was stopped at North Hudson. The troopers were sickened by the sight. Equally so was Lt. Alfred F. Crary, Zone 3 Commander, Troop B, called to the scene.

As accustomed as he was in his professional life to sights of what Man can inflict upon animals, Dr. Lopez was horrified. That feeling rapidly grew into a cold and furious anger.

The North Hudson episode was not the first involving animals carried on the super highway.

In 1976, for instance, two Canadians were arrested by State Police on cruelty charges. A search of their tractor-trailer revealed nearly 300 live calves being transported southward into the Albany area. Trooper Lawrence B. Bliss, Plattsburgh, made the arrests. It was reported that of 287 calves, more than 50 had fallen under their own weight and could not regain their feet, thus serving as a living carpet for the others. The two drivers were finded $25 each, released and told to return to Canada with their cargo.

In 1973 a trailer carrying 23 horses to Canadian death and eventual export to Europe, rolled over and eleven of the animals were killed. The driver, from Montreal, was arrested on a charge of cruelty to animals and received a fine.

The unbelievable carnage within the trailer is pictured, with carcasses of dead horses visible. While the photo may be a ghastly one to many, it is published to acquaint the public of conditions which existed during the horrendous trip.

—— State Police Photo

Before this incident, another driver was arrested on a similar charge when State Police saw legs of horses dangling like pieces of rope from a moving trailer, scraping and bouncing along the hard pavement as the truck moved onwards. It was found the floor of the trailer had given way and some of the animals had half-crashed through; broken legs were many; flesh had been torn from bone, and one horse was found trampled to death in the ensuing panic.

Even earlier, a Canadian who used a pasture a short distance south of the border, was arrested for failing to care for sick and infirm horses, also bound for butchery in Canada. The pastured animals, approximately 400 of them were found to be without adequate food and water. A spokesman for the company responsible bitterly criticized not only the Elmore Society for Prevention of Cruelty to Animals, which issued the complaint, but North Country newspapers for printing the story of hardship.

A spokesman was quoted:

"The newspaper had printed all those things and the animal society over there caused all that trouble for nothing. After all this was out in the open we had to work like hell to feed all those damn horses and everything. We could not do what we wanted on our own land that we had rented. They are our horses."

In this case, the individual concerned, who lived in Quebec, was fined $300 by a town justice, and ordered to take proper care of the animals. While the Elmore society was satisfied with the order to provide, members were not pleased at the slight fine.

The North Hudson episode of 1980, however, climaxed a growing feeling of frustration and anger over methods used by some in transporting horses to their doom. It was recognized that dealing in horses for the hippophagi of other countries, who delighted in their flesh, was a legal business.

"But," said one observer of the overall scene, "there is no reason under heaven that live animals must be treated as though they were already carcasses on the meat hook. Some of these animals were once pets, once treated well. Once loaded onto trucks, they are treated as though dead. The callousness shown is beyond belief."

The New York State Department of Agriculture and Markets law under which arrests were made, was considered not strong enough. A small fine was pittance to horse dealers whose loads, on occasion, might be worth as much as $40,000 or more. Horse flesh is big business.

There had to be a change in the law.

The North Hudson incident proved the catalyst. It aroused fury. It aroused public outcry. And it aroused deep disgust and dismay. The law was indeed changed, and how it came about is an interesting example of what John Q. and legislators can do if they work together. No problem is insurmountable if it is one Man has created.

When the trailer was stopped by State Police, horses were unloaded and remained at Frontier Town a few days, regaining strength. Not all made it. The horse in left foreground was too weak to stand while being fed. The horse stretched on the ground collapsed and perished. The death toll began to mount.

—— State Police Photo

27

Troopers Bob Carlson, Paul Manning and Ed Haroff, whose diligence while on patrol resulted in stopping the overladen trailer jammed with the dead and dying animals. Photo taken at Schroon Lake State Police headquarters.

I am personally grateful I had a small part to play in the change, since it evidences in positive fashion the part a newspaper can assume in instances of this nature.

When police and SPCA members found none of the original 85 horses stopped at North Hudson had had food or water, and that they had been driven from Florida and North Carolina with needs unfulfilled for an estimated three days, the survivors were quartered in a temporary corral through the courtesy of Frontier Town officials.

Here, for a short time, until further determination of their case could be made, they were given sustenance and medical attention. Some could barely stand. One Shetland pony in particular, was in agony; Dr. Lopez found one eye gouged out and hanging from its socket.

It is to the credit of many North Country residents that when the story got around — and this it did, with lightning speed — that a great deal of food was donated. It most assuredly is to the credit of Frontier Town, one of the best known tourist attractions in the Adirondacks, that total kindness replaced the brutality the horses had undergone.

Injuries suffered during the trip, as well as equine ailments afflicting the animals, accounted for the death of nineteen more as time moved on. Survivors were moved from Frontier Town to the Bruce Crammond farm at Ticonderoga where, under the expert care of the Crammond family, his workers, and Dr. Lopez, they regained strength slowly in their new freedom. One horse had been so mistreated it was promptly named "Bones." (This animal, sold later at an auction, gained approximately 300 pounds in a short time.)

The punishment for the two drivers of the truck? They were incarcerated in the Essex County jail at Elizabethtown for a short time, fined $150 each, and released.

I first heard about the incident at the Westport State Police station, where I stopped during a return trip from Plattsburgh a short time after the episode occurred. When I visited the Essex County jail to learn more details, I learned the drivers had been released. It was later that the full story began to unfold as described.

In a follow-up story days later, I wrote in The Times-Union:

"Brutal treatment of horses bound for death in a Canadian slaughterhouse, a pitiless and wild descent into horror for the animals which were jammed into a trailer without food or water for as long as three days, has aroused unprecedented fury throughout the eastern fringe of the Adirondacks.

"So much so, that the North Country Society for the Prevention of Cruelty to Animals has doubled efforts for an amendment to the State Department of Agriculture and Markets law which governs method of movement.

"Such an amendment has been offered in the past. The Assembly passed the bill; the Senate held it in committee for reasons unknown. It once again has been prefiled in the Assembly by Assemblyman Robert D'Andrea, Saratoga Springs, and State Senators Hugh Farley of Niskayuna and Joseph Bruno of Rensselaer County. Its fate remains to be seen."

This was written on January 18, 1981.

In actuality, while the bill was filed in the Assembly by D'Andrea, it had several cosponsors, including Albany's Dick Conners, Colonie's Michael Hoblock and Assemblywoman Joan Hague of the Town of Queensbury.

In essence, the bill established safety features for trailers, including elimination of sharp projections, adequate emergency exits, non-skid floors, loading ramps, adequate ceiling clearance and adequate ventilation. Every vehicle carrying more than six horses would have two doorways for ingress and egress, not on the same side.

Heavier fines were established for violators.

The bill is now law, and support was heavy.

While efforts for the new bill were being made, there remained the future of the survivors of the Torture Trail.

To claim them, the southern-based company handling the transportation faced claims which included feed and board as well as medical attention, costs which mounted daily despite donations. It soon became apparent that to reclaim the victims, the company would have to pay out more than they were worth.

Thus, after certain legal moves were made, a landmark decision in the United States occurred; the horses would be sold at auction. I am told this was the first decision of its kind made in the country under circumstances described.

There were legal expenses incurred by the SPCA in the matter of freeing the animals from bondage. A public appeal was made. It was well publicized. The response was prompt and generous; the North Country and Albany area together contributed approximately $3,000, which donations manifested the anger as well as sympathy of those contributing.

I have seldom seen a campaign of such spontaneity. Children responded as well as adults. One example: Dr. Lopez and his group received contributions from sixth graders at Schalmont Middle School, Duanesburg Road, Schenectady County, many miles to the south. With the donations was this comment from Craig E. Sargent, social studies teacher:

"Sixth graders have many things in common and one is the love for animals. Their contributions are from their hearts and we hope this legislation (the amendment mentioned) passes."

Bruce Crammond, on whose farm at Ticonderoga the landmark auction was held.

By January 26, 1981, about a month-and-one-half from the date the truck was stopped, $2,000 had been raised! And more arrived after that date. The response was tremendous. Letters and telephone calls reached this writer by the hundreds.

The way for an auction was finally cleared.

In the latter part of February, 1981, the surviving horses and ponies were considered well on their way to recovery; only one had succumbed. More than 300 interested buyers appeared at the Crammond farm under weather conditions which would have repelled most who attend outdoor auctions. It had rained steadily for four days; mud was inches deep, and Crammond had spread loads of straw and hay in and around the corral. Conditions deterred enthusiasm not one whit.

The fifty-five survivors, most of them remarkably active and spirited, many of them capable of being ridden, were auctioned off by representatives from the Cambridge Valley Livestock Market, Inc., Glenn McLenithan and George Tucker. So fast was the bidding that it was over in one hour and fifteen minutes. Prices paid ranged from a low of $30 to a high of $150 per animal.

Clarence Perry of Crown Point, with a pair of love-starved ponies which he purchased for his grandchildren, John and Shannon Stone. They didn't go unloved for long!

Folks came not only from New York State but from Vermont. A matched pair of ponies was purchased by Clarence Perry, Crown Point, for his grandchildren, John and Shannon Stone. I reported also that Mr. and Mrs. Patrick Donovan, Chilson, won the bid for a half-horse, half-pony, for their seven-year-old daughter Shannon Donovan.

Margaret Scuder, Ticonderoga, purchased three; Kelly Gough, Westport, left with a pony for nephew Dereck, seven, of Crown Point. The American Horse Protection Association, the only non-profit organization in the country dedicated to the welfare of horses, both wild and domestic, headquartered in Washington, D.C., bought two, including the Shetland which lost an eye. A sharp lookout was kept by James Provost of the Schenectady Animal Shelter and a Vice-President of the State Humane Association, as well as by others, to prevent "killers" from buying for the flesh market.

The sum raised was almost $5,000, less than half the amount which had been charged against the company for medical treatment, board and food and medicines. The animals, of course, had been released from quarantine because of medical and other attention given. Even though the sum did not cover expenses, Dr. Lopez said:

"We're satisfied. We kept them from the killers."

I wrote at the time that the survivors ate well during their convalescence. The Ticonderoga Equestrian Club, for instance, donated money for grain. The Lake George Produce Co. gave more than two tons of carrots. Some hay was donated, but most of the cost rested with Crammond and Dr. Lopez. Neither gentlemen received full value for services rendered, but both said emphatically:

"We are not in this for profit."

An interested observer at the auction was a man who viewed the entire proceedings with more than casual interest.

He was Trooper Ed Haroff of Schroon Lake. Troopers Carlson and Manning were unable to attend. Trooper Haroff, incidentally, owns his own stable, called Bar H, at Schroon Lake. At the auction, he observed, did not buy.

When I introduced him to an excited woman who had just purchased a pony, her eyes widened and she exclaimed:

"So you're one of those who helped!" Her reward was prompt; she threw her arms about the trooper and bussed him!

The auction ended, the crowd dispersed, leaving with new found pets. Adults and children alike led willing (if sometimes frisky) animals across the corn fields, ankle-deep in winter mud, to waiting vans. Others slogged through the mire after leaving instructions for delivery of their new additions.

The Torture Trail episode, from sadness at the beginning on December 12, to joy at auction's end, was over.

This Shetland pony, when rescued, was in pitiable condition. Its right eye had been gouged out during the trip. It was purchased at the February, 1981, auction at the Bruce Crammond farm in Ticonderoga, by the American Horse Protection Association and put to pasture and comfort in a safe haven in Virginia. The photo above, showing Gail Snider, AHPA's chief investigator, feeding a carrot to the animal, was taken by Trinket Doty. The pony has been named Lazarus. Photo used by courtesy of the AHPA.

Six of the horses auctioned off at the Crammond Farm were purchased by Arto Monaco of Upper Jay, seen above. Two more were sold to Lynda Denton, also of Upper Jay, his niece. A surprise awaited Monaco some time later when Diamond Lill, one of the mares, gave birth to Penny, pictured above in foreground. Penny, at birth, weighed only 25 pounds! As of this writing, all animals are doing fine; the tragic past, apparently, long forgotten.

Shannon Donovan, age 7 at the time of this photo, with her new possession, purchased by her parents, Mr. and Mrs. Patrick Donovan, Chilson.

32

The Bowman Saga

(continued)

As a Businessman, He Was Supreme;
As a Man Who Judged the
Future, He Was a Bust

The extraordinary story of John P. Bowman, the Stony Creek tannery tycoon of Warren County, who felt he would return to this world after death — (up to the present he has never made the trip) — was printed in vignette form in Adirondack Album, Volume 2.

It deserves elaboration.

I found, subsequently, there is more to the Bowman story than the brief paragraphs mentioned. I found also no chapter on the man could be complete without illustrations of the magnificent mausoleum he had constructed for himself and family, unusual even for the period in which he lived; almost a Pharaonic type of tomb of granite and marble which was very much part of his life.

In an Adirondack world filled with unusual historic figures, Bowman, a man of portly and dignified appearance, stands out as an idealist, theorist and capitalist.

He proved the existence of this unlikely combination. He was an idealist in his attitude toward his adored and adoring family; theorist in that he foresaw reincarnation where life, once extinguished, would be reborn and resume where it had been cruelly cut off. And he proved himself a capitalist in that he made a fortune.

Clarendon, Vt., was Bowman's birthplace; he greeted the world in January, 1815. After a growing up period, of which little is known, he left at age 15 to learn the tanning and currying (dressing of leather) trade in Rutland, Vt. That accomplished, he moved his unquestioned energies to New York State, at Hunter, Greene County, south of Albany, to learn the manufacturing end of producing sole leather.

From Hunter he went to Saugerties, Ulster County, and worked for B.A. Burhans.

A restless man, convinced that his future rested only in total control and ownership, he left that job after a few years and moved to Cuttingsville, Vt., a small community on Route 103, southwest of Rutland. Here, among Vermont hills, he opened his own manufacturing plant. In 1851 he was elected to the state legislature, but politics obviously palled because in 1852 he sold his business and crossed the New York State border once

again and settled in Stony Creek, a hamlet southwest of Warrensburg.

Bowman did what came naturally to many Vermonters at the time — sought fortune if not fame in New York State's wilderness region, then sparsely populated with scattered, small settlements, as well as with single-minded, rugged individualists who, having tasted what then was considered civilization, decided to live in hermitic, primitive and, at times, lawless style.

Such individuals were not murderers seeking solace among the whispering pines. Nor were they robbers, and they hardly could be termed thieves, since their own slim code of ethics forbade such.

They were men from various backgrounds who desired solitude and freedom, who felt the Adirondack areas in which they lived were places from which to pluck the necessities of life; they considered the mountains as an inexhaustible source of wildlife and killed not only for sustenance but for the ready markets to the south.

It was not unusual for scores of deer to fall to one man's gun over a period of a year. It was not unusual for deer to be clubbed to death while swimming desperately in a lake in which they had been driven by dogs. And it was not unusual for a half dozen or more bears to be trapped in huge iron jaws in less than a year.

Wildlife was cheap. There was no thought of tomorrow.

The Adirondack region, not yet the huge, six-million-acre park it is today, was still relatively free from the total ravages of lumbermen who felt God had made a tree for one purpose, to be felled, sliced by saw and sold.

The "great" days when in one downstream drive, more than 20 million feet of timber, board measure, would be floated down the old West Creek in the southern area of what today is designated as the West Canada Lake Wilderness Area, were yet to come. That magnificent drive in 1895 was ten years after the Forest Preserve came into being, and involved mostly spruce logs, cut on private property, much of which later was sold to New York State.

When Bowman arrived in Stony Creek in 1852, at age 37, he arrived with purpose. He purchased a tannery which needed completion. He had the money and the time. He put the tannery into shape and his rise to riches was rapid; at one time the enterprise turned out 40,000 sides of leather annually, a remarkable accomplishment, since both raw and finished hides had to be transported by horse teams to and from the railroad point in Saratoga Springs, an estimated 30 mile trip over roads which would defy a modern Army tank.

Nobody quite knows the workings of a man's mind, sometimes not even the man himself. Nobody knows just when this strange man's thoughts on an afterlife began to germinate. It is wonder, also, that he had time to mull such over.

He owned not only the tannery and his home, but 6,000 acres of timberlands, which included vast stands of virgin hemlock, the bark of which was used in the tanning process of the times.

At this period, incidentally, the eastern, or "Canada" hemlock, also known as the hemlock-spruce, which existed from Nova Scotia to Minnesota and southward to Maryland, was a much sought member of the pine family by tanners. Its bark contains tannates, or salts of tannic acid, with the ability to make skin fiber imputrescible — in other words, the leather defies putrefaction.

Hemlock at this time was considered inferior to spruce or pine and was not considered suitable for building purposes; that feeling has since changed. The tree grew to heights of 100 feet, with trunk diameter ranging from two to four feet.

Tanners looked at it only as a source of bark. Three to six hemlocks, depending upon size, containing approximately 1,000 feet of lumber, furnished only one cord of bark, and loggers could fill the demand for one year's supply by working only during a brief period — the only period possible, when the sap ran and bark could be peeled easily.

Bowman's woodsmen most assuredly did not practice scientific or managed forestry. The stately trees were cut, stripped naked on his property, and the lumber left to rot! His method, however, was no different from other tannery owners scattered through the Adirondacks. The one thing which saved the hemlock from almost total destruction was a new process in tanning, done without the need for bark.

Bowman married in 1849, three years before arriving at Stony Creek. He courted Jennie T. Gates, daughter of a Herkimer County resident, Franklin Gates, and the joining was fruitful; the couple had two daughters, Addie and Ella.

After amassing a fortune, the call of his native state proved too hard to resist. Bowman retired and with his family moved to Cuttingsville, scene of pleasant, younger and less pressurized days. There he constructed what has been described as an "elegant" Victorian mansion on Route 103. Directly across the dirt highway

he constructed a mausoleum which even today is considered a remarkable structure. Indeed, it is that in more than physical form. It contained his dreams. Today it remains a tourist attraction for thousands who roam Vermont countrysides. It is dated 1880.

It is located in the Laurel Glen Cemetery. The cost was an estimated $75,000, a huge sum for those days, and it is said more than 125 masons and sculptors worked for more than a year on its completion. Entombed within today are husband, wife, and daughters Addie and Ella.

Herein also rests the tragedy of Bowman's life.

Addie, his first child, died in infancy.

He received another emotional shock when in 1879 Ella, his second daughter, died in her early 20's.

Then came the worst blow of all. The following year his wife passed away.

Bowman stood alone.

In the building of the mausoleum, he ordered a sculpture of himself, larger than life, and this figure was placed on the steps leading to the entrance of the granite structure. He is displayed as grief stricken; a key is in his hand to open the door to his loved ones; he carries a mourning cloak, and holds a silk hat and wreath. The statue is remarkably life-like, as the illustrations will show.

Inside the tomb, visible through the iron grating stretching across the entrance, is the sculpture of a child, carved from marble, arms outstretched, reaching, it appears, for the embrace of mother and father. Behind the child is a bust, either of Mrs. Bowman or daughter Ella. There is an eeriness about the interior hard to describe. What can be described is that Bowman had determined he and his family would return; his statue is symbolic of that return.

Even as his wife and daughters were entombed in the vault, Bowman kept faith; kept the mansion and all rooms therein ready for their return. When he died in September, 1891, of a "combination of heart and lung trouble," at age 76, his will provided for a caretaker and a cook to keep the mansion in condition. The legend is that even linens were changed with regularity for the family's reunion!

It was not to be.

SEE PHOTOS
FOLLOWING PAGES

34

The scene at the Bowman mausoleum, photographed from a distance of several yards, showing the industrialist mounting the steps to join his family.

Late afternoon shadows are created as the camera gives a closer view of Bowman's bigger-than-life marble statue, before the grated entrance.

The fine detail of the sculpture is evident in this photograph; note even the eyes turned toward the door; key clasped in hand; the feeling of sorrow mirrored in stone on the man's face.

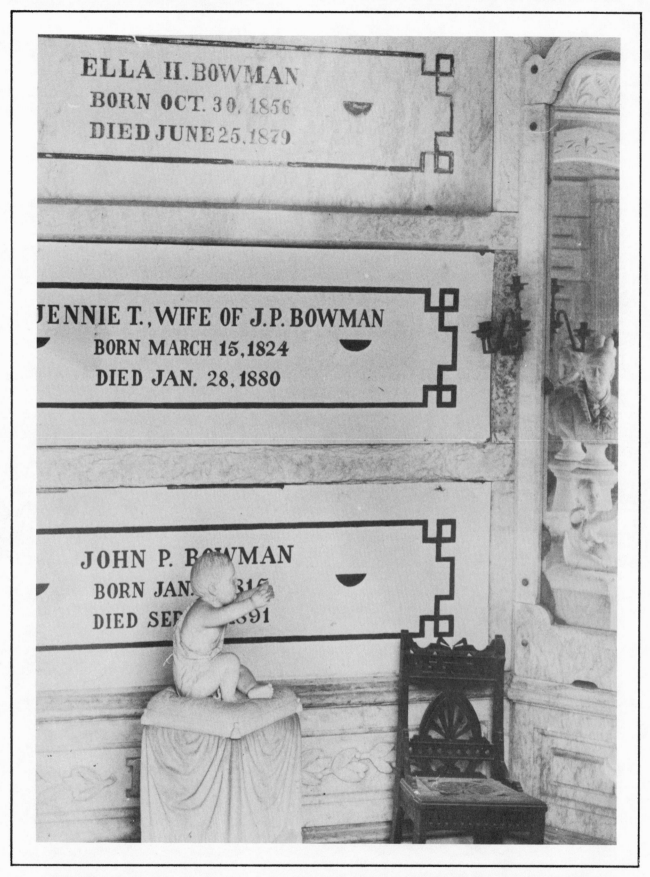

ELLA H. BOWMAN
BORN OCT. 30, 1856
DIED JUNE 25, 1879

JENNIE T., WIFE OF J.P. BOWMAN
BORN MARCH 15, 1824
DIED JAN. 28, 1880

JOHN P. BOWMAN
BORN JAN. 315
DIED SEP. 891

Stone likeness of Addie, the first born, who died in infancy, pictured in the tomb's eerie interior, with her reflection in a mirror at the right. Addie, born April 29, 1854, died on August 24, the same year. Her tomb rests above Ella Bowman, and was out of camera range. Note also reflection of bust of female member of the family in mirror.

Man-Made Miracle

It Was First A Lake, Then A
Swamp — Now It Is A
Lake Once Again, Serving
Many Purposes

A general view of the Conklingville dam and the Niagara Mohawk Power Corp. hydro-electric station.
Station is capable of producing 20,000 kilowatts; has a water drop of more than sixty feet to turbines.

There are bad monsters and there are nice monsters. Herewith offered examples:

Champy, the amiable Lake Champlain monster, is of the nicer variety, a solid citizen who minds his/her business and bothers nobody, and who merely uses Champlain as a giant waterbed in which to eat, sleep and swim. On occasion he/she has been known to gambol, which is not to be construed as a vice.

Joseph W. Zarzynski, Wilton, Saratoga County, foremost researcher of the Lake Champlain phenomenon, believes firmly in Champy's existence. On October 6, 1980, the Village of Port Henry, on the lake's shores, passed a resolution specifying that "all the waters of Lake Champlain which adjoin the Village of Port Henry are hereby declared to be off limits to anyone who would in any way, harm, harass or destroy the Lake Champlain Sea Monster."

A photo of what was described as Champy was snapped by a Connecticut housewife and was reprinted nationally. If the beast does not exist, it is the most publicized non-monster in the country.

So much for Champy and the likes of him/her.

Less amiable is the East Branch of the Ausable River at Upper Jay. This is a liquid monster and periodically it heaves and in rising it destroys. Its destruction of the Land of Make Believe, a tourist attraction, is widely known, is to be deplored.

In days gone by, Hudson's River was a monster and there was good reason. During snow melts and heavy rains in the mountains it gained awesome power; fed by tributaries, it overflowed its banks and the effects were felt as far south as Albany and Troy, where annual floods became a nightmare and rowboats replaced automobiles along its shores.

In the case of the Hudson, the monster has gone from bad to good. It has been tamed.

It has been tamed by construction of an earthen dam which, in turn, has formed what today is called the Great Sacandaga Lake, which herein shall be known as the Sacandaga Reservoir, because reservoir it is, and will remain. A rose by any other name is still a rose.

This big, man-made basin of fresh water, which can be likened in size to Lake George, located in both Saratoga and Fulton Counties, is now more than a half century old. It was born, literally, on March 27, 1930, when the gates at the Conklingville dam in Saratoga County were closed to the probing soft nose of the Sacandaga River, which river both feeds and empties the basin.

Huge it is; there are at least three hundred billion gallons of water which can be stored within its boundaries. Thus it becomes a placid giant withholding floods from the lower Hudson.

This fluid shroud of a former swampland, this tamer of the Hudson, is one that cloaks ancient secrets and historical shennanigans; it holds the memories of many still living and has buried the dreams of still thousands more.

Today, as a monument in an area often torn by drought, it is a living memorial to the memory of its designer and chief engineer, Edward Haynes Sargent, whose grave rests in a cemetery near Edinburgh, high above the huge lake he helped create.

Although born in 1930, the reservoir actually took longer in total creation; its massive acreage of 26,700 took a long time in filling. Thus it stands today, 52 years old, elderly in age, biologically speaking, but proved by time and contrast, for its creation has offered much in the way of argument for water impoundage.

In the year 1913, in March, for instance, eastern downtown Albany was knee deep in water and mud, brought there by a rampaging Hudson, which in its turbulent course southward, was joined by an equally turbulent Sacandaga River near Lake Luzerne. The marriage of the two made the Hudson great and Albany and Troy fearful.

Has the impoundage been successful?

Consider this: On New Year's day, 1949, nineteen years after the Sacandaga was held in the chains of the reservoir, a much greater flood than the 1913 version was prevented simply because the Sacandaga's waters were held at bay, to be released at will later by the Hudson River-Black River Regulating District, the reservoir's governing body, headquartered in Albany.

The district is a consolidation of the former Black River and Hudson River Regulating Districts under the laws of 1959. Three reservoirs are operated in the Black River area, including the Stillwater Reservoir on the headwaters of the Beaver River, and Old Forge and Sixth Lake Reservoirs on the Moose River, in the Towns of Webb, Herkimer County and Inlet, Hamilton County.

The Hudson River area includes the watershed above the Albany-Greene County line, exclusive of the area within the Mohawk River basin. It has an area of about 4,650 square miles, and the Sacandaga Reservoir is the only one so far constructed in the Hudson River area.

All this is a matter of history. And also a matter of history is the reservoir itself and how it grew.

In prehistoric times, ancient man roamed the region, and during these times a lake existed. Glacial action transferred the landscape into swamplands, and thus the great Sacandaga Vlei, or Vley, a gigantic marshland, was formed.

In historic times, Sir William Johnson, an Irishman who controlled the Indian destinies of the King of England in America, constructed a fishing and hunting lodge at Fish House, not only for the vigorous outdoor sports mentioned, but reportedly for more leisurely bedroom activities with not unwilling Indian maidens. In those days in the mid-1700's, unquestionably the wooded hills of the valley called "Sacondaga" by the Indians resounded with joyous hoots and howls of Johnson-sponsored gatherings of noted European emissaries who, under the influence of Adirondack dew momentarily forgot their continental dignity and partook of the more pleasant aspects of American primitive life.

Not so, of course, back in the 1600's, when the martyred Roman Catholic saint, Father Isaac Jogues, a prisoner and slave of the Mohawks from the village Ossernenon, near Fonda, helped his captors scour the great Vlei for the winter's supply of smoked fish. The swamp abounded in marine life.

In this same area during Revolutionary War days prowled the famous Nick Stoner, the Fulton County frontiersman, who one day appeared with a bale of furs and amiably reported to tavern buddies that he had acquired such by eliminating an Indian carrying the pack. True or not, it makes a good story.

One report has it that the swamp in early days encompassed as much as 5,000 acres, criss-crossed by more than twenty miles of streams, all fed, all mothered, by the Sacandaga, now all smothered in water and in deadly embrace by the same river. It was from this flooded Vlei that thousands of big northern pike swam to greater freedom as the reservoir's level began to rise, and it was from this growing lake that came the world's record northern, 46 pounds and three ounces of fighting flesh and bone, caught finally by the late Peter DuBuc, a former Albany resident. DuBuc caught the monster from shore on a September day in 1940, and I often tell the story to groups of the interview I had with the gentleman on the catch.

When I asked to see the mounting, DuBuc astonished me by saying it was not mounted.

He ate it!

You've heard that story before. It bears repeating.

DuBuc, in his seventies when I interviewed him, also told me that if he were feeling better, he felt there were more giants to catch. The gentleman, as I recall, had been injured when he assisted a woman driver stuck in snow.

It was in the reservoir also, that the late Steve LaFarr of Schenectady, a state diver of the helmet and rubberized canvas suit school, told me he often saw giant pike as he prowled the bottom of the lake as "big as

A desolate scene indeed, and one frequently met during the widespread drought of the 1960's. The reservoir was drawn thirty-three feet to minimum status and what was once underwater became naked and rock-strewn shoreline. The rise and fall of the reservoir has long been a bone of bitter contention; the battle for a more constant level continues even today.

torpedoes." And DuBuc himself, who knew Steve, recalled one instance when the diver surfaced from a job and asked for a knife because the northerns were nosing around his air line.

This was all part of the past in this big basin, which contained three small villages and eleven hamlets, miles of highway and telephone and power lines, along with 22 cemeteries going back in physical content to the 1700's.

Downstream floods proved to be problems not only in the twentieth century, but in the nineteenth. During the 1800's the State Legislature was petitioned for a series of dams to hold back the millions of tons of water that hammered communities.

It wasn't only Albany that felt the impact; Corinth and Glens Falls were hit by the angry Hudson as well. And it wasn't only the 1913 flood in Albany that finally touched off construction of the Conklingville dam; the entire $12 million project became a certainty when three flash floods hit downstream in 1922 and the Hudson River Regulating District was finally created by the state to do something about it all.

Not the world's record caught in the Sacandaga Reservoir, but a typical northern pike taken from that body of water. Powerful jaws are capable of pulling ducklings into oblivion.

In actuality, the overall plan called for storage reservoirs on the Hudson, Schroon, Indian, Sacandaga and Cedar Rivers and on several other tributaries, and the estimated cost ran about $30 million.

No state monies were involved in the Sacandaga construction; the cost was distributed among almost thirty industries and communities that had suffered long and hard from floods.

Creation of the big reservoir was no simple job. Many Adirondack impoundages were never cleared of trees, thus becoming graveyards for the forest; the Cranberry Lake basin is a prime example. A total of 12,000 acres of forest and field had to be cleared; 3,900 graves had to be relocated; villages and hamlets moved; highways rerouted, power and telephone lines set back. A railroad became a victim. The cost of removing timber alone, after land had been acquired, amounted to almost a million dollars. The land was cleared of stumpage and more than 5,000 stumps were removed near the villages of Northville and Sacandaga alone. This type of clearance also was a far cry from the creation of Indian Lake in Hamilton County to its present size in 1898, fed by the Jessup River, and which empties into Abanaki Lake and the Indian River, thus into the Upper Hudson.

During the walleyed pike spawning run in the spring, Cranberry Creek, above, one of the many smaller tributaries of the reservoir, is wall-to-wall with the fish, and such areas are heavily patrolled against poachers. Walleyes at this time can be literally scooped out of the creeks — or easily speared.

Work began on the Conklingville dam in 1927 and by 1930 the huge job was completed. It filled the Sacandaga gorge; the dam is more than one thousand feet in length and is one hundred feet in height; it is constructed of stone and earth and concrete and its inner core is of hardened granite dust. It holds back a reservoir miles wide between Mayfield and Northville.

The filling of the basin, whose waters are born in Sacandaga Lake and Lake Pleasant near Speculator, Hamilton County, took time; after the gates were closed at Conklingville, it took more than a year to reach proper level.

At low water, such as during the devastating drought period during the 1960's, a portion of the past is disclosed in narrow roads, in foundations of homes and other buildings. The reservoir acts not only to impound flood waters, but is a source of hydro-electric power for the Niagara-Mohawk Power Corporation. If the reservoir prevents floods, it is also used to maintain minimum flows in the Hudson during dry periods. The reservoir cannot be drawn below a certain level; the law requires the existence of what is known as a "conservation pool," that is, a pool of sufficient depth to maintain marine life.

Admittedly difficulties arose after the basin was filled. Summer vacation camps along the shoreline are permanently fixed in location. The water level goes up and down; this causes problems with docks and boating. Shoreline residents have been, and probably will be for time to come, at odds with the regulation board over maintenance of water levels. Thus there is the battle between those seeking recreation and those who seek power and flood control. The two sides probably will never come to total agreement.

At one time, not too many years ago, one argument used by those who favor a steady level, suggested that instead of the reservoir releasing water for maintenance of a steady flow in the Hudson, that Indian Lake be tapped. A howl of protest resulted, since Indian Lake has its own problems.

However, one thing remains constant as the years roll on. The reservoir has served its purpose well. Albany and Troy no longer look forward to floods; fish no longer glide over the lands of eastern Albany. The upper Hudson's level is kept constant, or reasonably so for benefit of industry downstream. The Sacandaga River itself has been tamed. Power continues to be generated as waters permit.

In the overall picture, this is what was desired, and is what has been done.

ADDITIONAL SACANDAGA
PHOTOS ON FOLLOWING PAGES

The fury of an unleashed Hudson is evident in the photos on this and the succeeding page. Pictures taken in 1913 at Glens Falls, showing the bridge between S. Glens Falls and Glens Falls as it was, and what happened when raging floodwaters took their toll. Such "incidents" led to the creation of the dam at Conklingville, a project designed to tame the Sacandaga River.

Homes were moved to make way for the rising waters. This two-story structure was jacked off its stone foundation and rolled to a new location on logs. Note vintage car and wagon at lower right.

Another scene of sadness; home owners piling belongings from a home to be demolished in the Batchlerville area. A portion of the original bridge, then under construction, may be seen in the background.

Pictured is a construction stage of the hydro-electric plant at Conklingville dam during the early 1930's. The reservoir, incidentally, does not maintain a constant level for power purposes. The Hudson River demands flow to maintain that stream's level; recreation makes further demands and, of course, drought itself can create problems. The reservoir surface, when full, is 768 feet above sea level, and it cannot be drawn lower than 735, which means a fluctuation of thirty-three feet is possible.

Old and New

Demolition and construction are pictured in this photo, taken while the original Batchlerville bridge was being built — a span which was ~~replaced~~ *repaired* in 1982 after years had taken their toll. Note homes partially stripped as the waters of the reservoir continued their inexorable rise.

The new span at Batchlerville while under construction. While building went on, a ferry service was instituted — for passengers only. Photo was taken by Skip Dickstein of Capital Newspapers.

Another example of what happens when the waters are drawn for power or to feed Hudson's River. Docks on drums descend with diminishing levels, infuriating owners of shoreline camps and cottages.

While the Sacandaga River may, on occasion, become a wild and woolly stream, it has placid moments. Shown is the river bed during the long drought of the 1960's when, astonishingly, water became a precious commodity in the North Country. Photo taken downstream from Wells, Hamilton County.

The dam at what is known as Stewart's Bridge, downstream from Conklingville, another hydro-electric complex operated by Niagara Mohawk. This was built in 1952; is capable of producing 30,000 kilowatts; the drop of water to turbines is about one hundred feet. Water, instead of oil or coal, is thus used twice. It is interesting to note that on the Raquette River sixteen hydro plants operate, thus using the same waters that number of times!

Adirondack Wildlife - Fact and Fancy

Sad to say, no one paid much attention to the detailed study of animals in the Adirondacks prior to the 1800's and during an early portion of the nineteenth century.

Peter Kalm, the Swedish naturalist who traveled through the North Country during the mid-1700's, does mention a variety, but seems to be more concerned in the discomforts of such flying predators as the black fly and the mosquito. That, of course, is a matter of personal opinion, open to argument.

The animals were in the Adirondacks during the days when the white man moved into the region. And they were killed for meat or sport. Invading armies on the eastern fringe not only observed wildlife, but devoured what they saw and shot.

The same situation existed insofar as fish or birdlife were concerned. When trout were desired in quantity during the days when tourists began to move into the region, their habitat was dynamited and they were collected by the hundreds, their fried or broiled remains placed on menus. When meat was desired, the whitetails were shot by the thousands, at any season, at any time of day or night.

The game seemed inexhaustible; venison was shipped to such summer resorts as Saratoga Springs, by the wagonload. In the Catskills, the deer were wiped out, and the area was later restocked with animals from the Adirondacks.

The variety of mammals known to exist in the entire state in 1842 was fifty-six. In 1899, as studies continued, the list of mammals existing within New York State jumped to eighty-one, but the list included occupants of what was considered as "state water," including ocean shoreline, and included the harbor porpoise, sperm whale, as well as the eastern wapiti or elk and the moose. One can add the black rat, house rat, panther, wolf and even the wolverine.

Donaldson, in his "A History of the Adirondacks," published in 1921, lists only fifty varieties as living or having lived in the Adirondacks, and the list includes the harbor seal (probably in Lake Champlain), as well as the wolverine, lynx, wolf and panther. He also listed the fossil elephant and the fossil horse, but one must gather such beasts haven't been seen around the mountains since Noah launched the world's best known barge.

Admittedly some of these animals are gone from not only the Adirondacks but the state. The wolverine is one example. The timber wolf and panther are considered extinct by some. Moose, largest of the deer family, are wanderers from elsewhere — or are they? The same might be said about the panther, or puma, and the timber wolf. Have any returned to the more primitive wilderness areas of the mountains? We know the coyote has expanded its range. Have others?

Any list of mammals of the region under discussion includes, of course, large and small varieties. If the bear is to be mentioned as a resident, so must be the dusky and red bat, the jumping mouse, meadow mouse and the familiar white-footed mouse. And don't forget the moles and the short-tailed shrew!

Insofar as birds are concerned, more than one hundred and fifty varieties of "easily found" birds are listed in Donaldson's work, as permanent or summer residents. However, a more up-to-date number is furnished by John M.C. Peterson of Elizabethtown, a past president of the High Peaks Audubon Society chapter. A chapter survey has revealed one hundred and eighty-five varieties of breeding birds — ones which nest in the Adirondacks. And that list is being expanded under a current study, which as of this writing has recorded many more.

This includes a comparative newcomer, the turkey vulture, which is moving up from the South; one was observed in 1980 with a tag showing it had flown from Miami, Florida! Peterson feels the species may become permanent residents before too many years have passed.

At any rate, no volume about the North Country is quite complete without adequate mention of wildlife. The whitetails are just as much part of the region as are Mt. Marcy or Whiteface Mt. So is the bear, the state record of which was shot in the mountains. The last elk was shot in 1946 — and that probably was one of a group brought in for restocking purposes. None has been seen since.

When one envisions wilderness, one must include those who live in it, without exception. Therefore this note is added, almost in the form of a riddle:

"From a taxonomic point of view, he is without any doubt a chordate, for a notochord, gill slits, and a hollow dorsal nerve cord appear during the course of his embryonic development, just as they do in the life of a fish, a frog, a lizard, a hen and a cat. He has a jointed backbone and so is a vertebrate; he has warm blood, hair and an abdomen, and so is a mammal."

I include this description because the mammal just described happens to be Man as portrayed by a biologist!

Man, in this volume, is most assuredly not listed as a biological specimen, but as the ruler of the vast Adirondack domain.

What is described, sometimes fancifully, on subsequent pages, is a selected list of more common four-legged animals and few comments on birdlife.

Most are present day inhabitants; some are open, as previously discussed, to question. But Nature is not a static personality. She has her whims. And who is there to stoutly say that the wolf, the panther and the moose, as examples, are to remain extinct forever in the rugged terrain so many tramp and adore?

The coyote is here to stay; it is a familiar predator not only in the Adirondacks but has invaded more settled areas. While it may occasionally kill a sick or deer made helpless by weather or injury, its main supply of food is drawn from smaller animals, such as rabbits and mice.

Bodacious Behemoth of the Back Country

Fish stories have held the spotlight far too long. It is time to replace the subject matter with fur instead of scales.

Your attention is respectfully drawn to an instance which occurred in the Lake Colden area of the North Country, when a gentleman was awakened one night by a noise outside his cabin.

He directed a spotlight to the area and saw a female bear (sow) which had managed to maneuver nose-first into one of his pork barrels. He promptly peppered her well-padded rump with a shotgun and the bear, astonished at this remarkable display of discourtesy, went right smack through and took off — with the barrel still wrapped around her body, twixt her front and rear legs.

As it usually does, time passed.

Same cabin. Same man. Another noise of the night. This time, bathed in light, was the same bear, still wearing the barrel. She had company. Two cubs.

And both wore small kegs around their little bellies.

Belief remains up to the reader.

Bear stories abound. They should. The animal is one of the most unusual inhabitants of the Adirondacks. It has a temper. Outbursts are unpredictable. It eats almost everything, from fat grubs to carrion. Its favorite haunts are in mature forests, but it is no stranger to community dumps. It walks, runs, swims and climbs trees.

It is a powerhouse of muscle. One student of the beast told me that pound for pound, it is the strongest animal on the North American continent. One blow from the paw of an infuriated bear would immobilize the top ten human heavyweights of the world. Its claws, non-retractable, are enormous and capable of tearing stumps apart.

In swimming, it usually points its snout at a specific point letting nothing interfere with its course. It is said a swimming bruin travels in such a straight line that in days long gone Indians stood in the shallows near the shore with stone axes or spears waiting for the victim to swim into striking range.

A former New York State zoologist, canoeing a pond in Maine one day found himself in a direct route of a mother and two cubs. When she spotted the canoe, she slowed for the cubs to catch up, waited while they fastened their claws into her thick fur and towed them to shore. The zoologist wisely changed course.

Early records reveal that on occasion when Indians did not change the course of their own craft, the bear merely barged into it, dumping the occupants.

The bear, which is native not only to the Adirondacks but the Catskills, is of Dr. Jekyll and Mr. Hyde aspect; it is an off-size mastodon at times, clown or killer, extrovert or hermit, depending entirely upon his/her mood. The black bear of the state is considered untamable. There have been instances of bears chained to stakes, turning upon their keepers, hugging them like a vise, holding them close with one forepaw and shredding an arm into sphagetti.

The average weight of animals shot in the state seldom runs more than 180 pounds; many run 150 or less. This is in contrast to the old days. Average live weight of 121 bears shot in 1906, for instance, was 174 pounds and six were more than 400. Twelve were between 300 and 400, which is a lot of sow or boar, whatever the sex.

Earlier, in 1904, eleven of about 150 bears shot in the Adirondacks weighed more than 300 pounds, and the largest scaled 428.

In 1938 Jean Mose of Saranac Lake killed a 532-pounder.

The big ones are still around, although less in number.
The largest ever killed in New York State was toppled in the Adirondacks. It was taken by Edward Ball of Batavia, Genesee County, on Sept. 13, 1975, in the Town of Altamont, Franklin County. This trophy, thirty-two years old, was weighed at Hurli Bros., Lake Placid. Live weight was 750 pounds. Dressed weight (entrails removed) was 660 pounds. It was killed by a shotgun slug.

It broke the weight record held by Richard Muhlig, White Sulphur Springs, Sullivan County, who on Sept. 14, 1974, also shot a male in the Town of Inlet, Hamilton County. This boar was nine-and-three-quarters years old; live weight was an estimated 655 pounds, and dressed, the carcass weighed 575. A rifle was used.

Muhlig's bear topped the previous record shot by Robert Avery in the Town of Benson, Hamilton County, in 1962. This one was a 562-pound boar.

Age? The Adirondack black is relatively long-lived. In 1958 a thirty-two-and-three-quarter-year-old was killed in the Town of Hopkinton, St. Lawrence County. But this was topped when Milton C. York of Corinth, Saratoga County, while hunting in the Town of Newcomb, Essex County, shot a boar forty-one-and-three-quarters years old, currently the state record for longevity.

Bear age can be ascertained by a technique developed by biologists in New York State. A microscopic inspection of a bear's teeth reveals "annual growth rings in the cement," which helps anchor the tooth into the jaw. The method is similar to ascertaining the age of a tree by counting growth rings.

Sexual activity? Both sows and boars reach maturity between 2.5 and 3.5 years of age, and first matings usually occur at this time. The breeding period is brief, with most activity in June.

But the black bear is an animal which exhibits a reproductive phenomenon called "delayed implantation."

The process is described in a detailed article on the species, written as a Cornell University publication. The authors are Daniel J. Decker, John O'Pezio, John W. Kelley, Gary R. Goff and Ronald A. Howard Jr.

I quote:

"When mating occurs, the eggs are fertilized and the zygote (fertilized egg) begins the process of cell division but does not grow beyond the blastocysts stage (hollow ball of cells). The embryo does not attach to the wall of the uterus or continue to grow until late fall. Cubs are born between mid-January and early February. Thus during the gestation period, which is about 220 days, actual fetal development only occurs during the last ten weeks or so."

The idea of a 750-pound black bear may cause amazement. The reason, of course, is that at birth, the young not only are blind, almost hairless, but are about the size of a red squirrel! Their weight would be between six and ten ounces each. Twins or triplets are common litter size, but there have been instances of six.

Although weighing only ounces at birth, by the time the cubs leave their den with Mama in early spring, they will weigh from five to fifteen pounds each, which demonstrates vividly the fact that it pays to stay around Mama's apron strings.

The cubs are weaned when they are about eight months old; den with the mother during the first winter and upon emergence in the following spring will weigh an estimated 55 pounds each.

The family splits in June when the sow becomes sexually active once again. Females will not breed while nursing; thus the production line is active every other year. Nature, being the lady she is, holds compensation if the cubs die in early spring. The mother may breed during consecutive years. This in itself, is a phenomenon and is evidence of the manner in which Nature perpetuates the species.

In numbers, black bears obviously feel the Adirondack Park is the place to live and love. Estimates place the population at a bit more than 3,500, as opposed to the Catskills, where the number is considerably less. But, then, it must be remembered that the Catskill area was settled earlier than the North Country and both the bear and the deer were once wiped out.

State record black bear, above, was shot by Edward Ball of Batavia, on Sept. 13, 1975. Its age of 32 years was determined by pre-molar analysis. The animal was killed in the Town of Altamont, Franklin County: its live weight was 750 pounds.

Ball's trophy broke the previous record held by Richard Muhlig of White Sulphur Springs, Sullivan County, who shot a boar in the Town of Inlet, Hamilton County, on Sept. 14, 1974. It weighed 655 pounds, was almost ten years of age, is pictured at left.

In the Adirondacks the bounty system, instituted in 1892, cut the number drastically. In that year, New York State posted a $10 bounty, and it was repealed three years later. Almost one thousand bears were slaughtered during that period. Bounties were paid on 359 bears in the North Country alone. By 1894, the estimated population in both the North Country and Catskills was 1,500.

Official protection, that is, limited seasons, came in 1903, and killing black bears during July, August and September was prohibited. A semblance of game management came into existence when successful hunters were required to file reports with the Forest, Fish and Game Commission, which preceded the Department of Environmental Conservation. Protection continued and seasons were shortened.

Mention has been made of eating habits. The digestive process is a marvel of Nature. The bear will eat both plant and animal life. The estimate offers this unusual breakdown: Plant life, seventy-five percent; carrion, fifteen percent; insects, seven percent, and small mammals such as mice, squirrels and rats make up most of the rest. Amphibians do not escape oblivion; frogs are devoured. Bruin has been known to eat housecats foolish enough to come within his reach and pet dogs have fallen victims as well.

The blacks like berries. They like acorns and beechnuts. They also eat deerberry, grapes, chokeberry, mountain ash, clover, red cedar leaves, pine needles, yellow birch seeds, dogwood buds, dandelion seeds, maple seeds, sumac, roots, bulbs and skunk cabbage, the latter a delicacy, dim as it may sound.

They are good at fishing, using paws as scoops. They'll spend hours digging up a woodchuck apoplectic with terror. They will spend more hours in profound contemplation as they run down ants with their tongues. They love apples and often get drunk on fermenting juices.

While their natural enemies are panthers, wolves, porcupines and humans, the former two no longer constitute menace, and the porcupine may only occasionally cause death when its quills block normal eating habits. Humans remain and humans represent the only force to hold the population in check; without annual takes, the bears would become a major nuisance, far greater than they represent today. They are susceptible to such diseases as tuberculosis, anthrax and pneumonia but according to biologists, disease seldom takes a toll.

The bear is probably best known for its attack on apiaries. No one realizes what damage looks like until he has seen an apiary clawed clean of honey by a hungry bear. A destroyed apiary makes a town dump look like a residential area. For some reason, the ammunition of bees doesn't seem to affect bruin unduly. I watched one at work on some hives, surrounded literally by thousands of indignant insects. Occasionally he would grunt like a pig in a trough and casually wave a honey laden paw to brush the nuisances away. Beekeepers have been

Typical "bear stump." Half-rotted remains have been clawed by a black bear in its search for grubs and insects. Sight is not uncommon in bear country.

known to shoot to kill in such instances. And one individual along the Canadian border poisoned a maurauder with a piece of pork laced with strychnine.

In early days, lumberjacks were known to strike until raiding bears were killed off.

Dens, that is, locations where they spend the winter, can consist of caves, windfalls, or can be built in thick balsam thickets — any spot where there is shelter. While many refer to the winter period as one of hibernation, this is not fact; the bear is not a true hibernator; the body temperature drops about ten degrees and remains reasonably constant.

One reason it is able to do so is the layer of fat accumulated before denning up. Fat may be as much as four to five inches thick and in one instance, a hunter measured a seven-inch layer around the neck and shoulders! Such proves a reservoir which is drained as the need arises.

Oddly enough, during the denning period, which may last up to a half year in New York State, a bear will not eat, will not drink, and will not defecate. Digestive organs contract. No food moves through the gastrointestinal tract simply because a "plug" forms in the intestines, formed of leaves or other woodland substances! Obviously the "plug" quickly disappears when the animal becomes active.

All in all, bruin is quite a package, but his day as a much sought-after game animal is long gone. If pressure exists today it is not mainly for the meat, but for the hide, the desire to possess a bearskin rug.

In the early days, when England ruled, bears were priced high; the hides were shipped to England where they were made into shakos, a form of head adornment, or small capes.

Regardless of ultimate use, the unpredictable black bear of the Adirondacks remains and will remain as one of the big game animals of the forest.

The two photos are included for comparison. Black bear is pictured at left. Above, alert to the camera, is a grizzly, as unpredictable in action as a black. Both are in prime shape, ready for winter. The grizzly does not inhabit the eastern United States. Note odd stance of the grizzly, with its paws crossed.

A remarkable photo, taken of black bears in the mating act, a sight seldom seen, a sight even less seldom recorded on film.

There are bear stumps and there are bear trees. A black bear, at right, is in the process of marking the tree with his sign. Some say it represents territorial domain, others say it keeps the animal's claws in shape. Whatever, it shows the power of these weapons.

At left is the scene presented after a bruin has marked his tree. The wounds in this instance are approximately one yard in length.

Sow black bear and cubs. Bears, even the young, are expert climbers. A bear often will settle comfortably in the crotch of a beech tree and from this position will reach out for branches with its paws, drawing them within reach of its mouth. In this way the animal gathers a favorite food, beechnuts. A mother bear, incidentally, with cubs, is no animal to approach or tease.

The "Gray Menace"

The story goes — and one may question its veracity but not its drama — that long ago, during the 1800's in the Indian Lake section of the Adirondacks, on a cold and moonlit winter's night, a staunch Adirondacker left the local store after purchasing supplies, boarded his horse-drawn sleigh, and off he went homewards through crusty snow, through woods and fields.

Like other mountain men he possessed a rifle; like others he carried it for a prime reason; predators such as the timber wolf, a rangy and powerful brute, roamed the region. A sweating horse, as well as the man who drove it, might prove a tempting bait.

Under the star-studded sky the trip was uneventful until the faintly marked road entered a long, open stretch. It was at this point terror became a companion. Distinct were the sounds of a wolf pack in full pursuit. There was no doubt of the pack's objective once the first big beast burst from the forest like a banshee, followed by fifteen other gray devils of the same make and model.

The horse proved no match for speed in the snow; its hoofs went through the crust while the wolves ran lightly over it. The leader was almost upon the sleigh when the man turned, shot it dead.

An astonishing happenstance thereupon occurred. The pursuit ceased while the starved pack leaped upon the fallen leader and devoured him in a matter of minutes. The grim chase then resumed with zest. The leader, so discourteously gobbled, had merely proved an appetizer.

There developed, in this race for life, a pattern. As the frenzied animals advanced, new leaders appeared from the pack and assumed their places in the front. Each time the terrified man shot a leader, its companions stopped only long enough to pay last respects by removing all visible traces.

Within a short time the pack had shrunk to five. And while the remaining wolves were understandably heavier, and thus less able to keep up the original pace, the horse was also wearying fast and had diminished its own strides. The battle thus continued with the man shooting each new leader as it appeared.

Finally there were only two.

Despair crushed the man as he fished his pockets for more shells; sweat cascaded from his forehead as he found he had only one! The lead wolf, bulging, white fangs bared to bloodied gums, was almost upon him. Into the beast slammed the last bullet. The animal dropped. The remaining wolf fell upon the carcass. The man whipped the horse furiously but that noble animal, drained of energy, flopped helplessly in the snow.

The man faced the remaining wolf with empty gun, still miles from help. And he felt he was too young to die. He was only eighty. The wolf felt otherwise. After polishing off its buddy, it staggered slightly, then lifted its massive, slit-eyed head in a long, hard and calculating look.

It was at this point that inspiration touched the octogenarian. Reaching into his groceries, he plucked therefrom a pork chop. Holding this tid-bit in one hand, the empty gun in the other, he approached the wolf, waving the chop under its flared nostrils, readying the rifle as a club, ready to fight a fight of awesome violence before leaving for that Great Adirondack Valhalla in the Sky reserved for senior citizen warriors.

But the trip wasn't necessary.

The wolf, tottering, took one despairing sniff, groaned piteously and from its depths thundered a gargantuan belch. The astonished man leaped back. Seconds later, loaded with fifteen of its companions, the beast exploded in a roar heard throughout the mountains. Housewives miles distant cringed. Brave men grew steely-eyed and dashed for their most prized possessions, their rifles.

They still say that the next day folks picked up pieces of wolf a mile away.

And, happily, the man reached the century mark. Well . . . .

The current attitude toward the wolf is a mixed one. Movies and TV continue to portray the animal as a brute of utter ferocity toward animal and human alike. Yet there is a growing feeling that the brush has painted the wolf too black. Admittedly it is merciless in hunting, but so is any carnivore. The world of the wild is not exactly filled with supermarkets where food can be obtained. To eat, the animal must kill. And killing is not a delicate procedure. Ask anyone who has seen a dog pack tear a deer to pieces, not for eating, but for sport.

A wolf can become a pet. It will evidence dog tactics when pleased. This writer knows of several individuals who own near purebreds and they have become tame and faithful. They most assuredly are no stranger to Man, having been associated with him from Neanderthal days; as a matter of fact, the domestication of the wolf began in prehistoric days when Man began to realize the predator could help in hunting.

Yet this unusual animal, which can go without eating for as long as eighteen or twenty days, and regain most of his weight after two or three hearty meals, seems to have touched off terror in the average human. I guess, in a way, Little Red Riding Hood must have started the ball rolling as far as popular opinion is concerned. So be it.

Some say the timber wolf is gone from the Adirondacks today, but is it really? Some say the last one was shot in 1899 in St. Lawrence County. Was it? A decade or so ago a true timber was seen in the Caroga Lake area of Fulton County. Shortly thereafter it met an ignoble fate; it was killed by an automobile. The skull was sent to a federal wildlife research lab in Washington. The report came back: The skull was that of a timber wolf.

With vast areas of the mountains now designated as wilderness areas, where no motorized traffic is permitted, might not these tranquil regions draw the timber back to its once native haunts? Or is the wolf to be forever replaced by the ubiquitous coyote, now firmly entrenched? Interesting thought, since other species, once considered extinct, have returned. The Fulton County animal was thought to have been an emigrant from Canada. Have others followed?

The timber wolf, (Canis lupus), is no midget. He is heavily built, can reach one hundred pounds or more; is designed for destruction, endurance and speed, and is feared by man and animal alike. The timber will reach lengths of five-and-one-half to six feet, including the tail, which may account for about twelve inches.

History is filled with mention of wolves. One of the most interesting is in a diary kept by Joshua Phineas Goodenough, a private with Rogers Rangers in the mid 1700's, when that corps was serving in the Adirondack region.

He told of a disturbing incident in 1755 when he was on a scout from Fort Edward in Washington County. A slow, two-day march from that French and Indian War fort on the Hudson brought his party into the general area of Fort Ticonderoga, (then Fort Carillon), then being constructed on hostile (French) territory. On the second night Joshua's party was awakened by gun shots and the howling of wolves.

"We decided," he wrote, "that the firing could not come from a large party and so began to approach the sound slowly and with the greatest caution. We could not understand why the wolves should be so bold with the gun firing, but as we came nearer we smelled smoke and knew it was a campfire.

"There were a number of wolves running about in the underbrush and from a rise we could presently see the camp and were surprised to find it contained five Indians all lying asleep in their blankets.

"The wolves would go right up to the camp and yet the Indians did not deign to give them any notice whatsoever, or even to move in the least when one wolf pulled at the blanket of a sleeper. We each selected a man, and prepared to deliver our fire, when all of a

61

sudden one figure rose up slightly. We nevertheless fired and then rushed forward, reloading.

"To our astonishment none of the figures moved in the least but the wolves scurried off. We were advancing cautiously when Shanks Shankland (another Ranger) caught me by the arm, saying 'We must run, that they had all died of smallpox,' and run we did, lustily for a long distance.

"After this manner did many Indians die in the wilderness from that dreadful disease and I have since supposed that the last living Indian had kept firing his gun at the wolves until he had no longer strength to reload his piece."

(This so-called "Smallpox Scout" of the Rangers reveals a rather interesting sidelight into Adirondack history. It is probable this disease, picked up from the whites, killed more Indians than all other causes combined).

Pvt. Goodenough, incidentally, seems to have developed an affinity for wolves. On another scout, under orders not to fire at game, he found himself standing by a tree during a snow storm with his gun under his blanket. Chancing to glance about, he saw a large wolf "just ready to spring." Fortunately another ranger happened by, scaring off the wolf and Goodenough did not find it necessary to disobey the order.

Then, too, there is the fascinating "Journal of a Hunting Excursion to Louis Lake, 1851," an Adirondack Museum publication, describing a jaunt by New York sports. Louis Lake is now known as Lewey Lake; is between Speculator and Indian Lake. The journal was kept by a party member. The group journeyed up Hudson's River by boat, boarded a train for Amsterdam, then went north to Northville and into the Speculator area by stage in September. On their last day, while fishing Lewey Lake for trout, it began to rain. A quote from the journal:

"What greatly accelerated our return (to the shanty) also, was the inconveniently near approach of a pack of wolves, whose conversation being conducted in a rather boisterous manner, greatly disgusted us with their behavior."

(The behavior of the party members was not exactly above reproach. During their trip members had run deer into Lewey Lake with dogs and pursued and killed the whitetails while helpless in the water).

Other Adirondack writers have often mentioned the animals. William Chapman White, in his "Adirondack Country," tells of a Ticonderoga woman who first came to that village in 1797, and who said it was impossible to keep sheep.

Wolves are believed to have roamed throughout the entire state, although there is surprising disagreement. Morse's Universal Geography, published in 1793, said:

"In the northern and unsettled parts of the state are plenty of moose, deer, bears, some beavers, martins and most other inhabitants of the forest except wolves."

Yet in a history of Saratoga County, it was pointed out that in the late 1700's Adam Comstock journeyed to Wilton from the area now known as South Corinth, for provisions of pork. The account, published in 1878, says Mr. Comstock made his return trip at night but eventually spent darkness straddling a boulder. Reason: Wolves had scented the meat and gathered 'round. He chose a sapling as a weapon and spent the night beating them off. They disappeared with advent of dawn.

One can go back even more distant in time.

Rev. Johannes Megapolensis Jr., an early Dutch preacher, describing the Mohawk Indians and their forest lands, said:

"I have also eaten here several times of elks, which were very fat and tasted much like venison; and besides these profitable beasts we have also in this country lions, bears, wolves, foxes and particularly very many snakes which are large and as long as eight, ten and twelve feet."

The snakes mentioned were rattlers, new to the early Dutch.

Bounties on wolves had been in existence within the state itself for a long time — in 1663, for instance, when wolves plagued Jamaica, Long Island, it was agreed that "whosoever kills any wolf, the head being shown to the Town or nailed on a tree, shall have seven bushels of Indian corn."

Nailing wolf heads for evidence of kills reached a peak in 1665, when the Town of Flatlands, L.I., awarded "the value of an Indian coat" to the person who killed a wolf and so proved the feat to a constable. The head was nailed on the constable's door!

The probable reason for attaching the head to the door of a lawman was to prevent its reuse by some rascals. Such reuse of trophies for bounties was not uncommon then or later. Larceny seizes upon no specific decade.

From 1820 to 1822, Franklin County nimrods astonished the hunting world by applying for more than $55,000 in bounties — at $60 a head, and this represented the combined state and county sums. It took a shaken state legislature in Albany to cure this massive attack upon the wolf and upon municipal coffers, and this it did by specifying that ears had to be removed and burned at once by the accepting officer. It was quite obvious that whole wolf heads were being recycled for hard cash.

The ceaseless killing, whether for bounty or sport, continued until by 1899 the state could report that:

"While the wolf formerly ranged throughout the state, it is now exterminated everywhere except in the wildest parts of the Adirondacks."

Man, in this instance, issued the statement.

Nature remained and remains mute.

But, then, she always does when she's got a surprise up her sleeve. It is highly probable she may get angry enough to plan and carry out the wolf's comeback.

It could happen.

62

Paul Crear of Crear Farm, Severance, north of Schroon Lake, has owned "Wolf," a pet seven-eighths wolf, and one-eighth dog, for twelve years. The family pet came from the Canadian Northwest; is affectionate, faithful, and demostrates the fact that the wolf strain can be domesticated to the point where a gentle giant can become a gentle pet.

Mr. Cute-
The Killer

In this excellent work of art, drawn by Clayt Seagears, former director of the Division of Conservation Education, EnCon, a mother red squirrel is engaged in a bit of gory work – teaching her offspring the "art" of killing a nestful of a vireo's brood. The reds excell in the art of bird destruction. Drawing appeared in The Conservationist Magazine.

Difficult to acknowledge if one is an animal lover is that the common red squirrel, also known as the pine squirrel or chickaree, is one of the greatest killers of birds.

One statistic offered by a student of the beast is frightening: Each red can be held responsible for the death of 200 birds each season!

The killing is not only of the young, but in the destruction of eggs in the nest. The statistic can become even more perturbing when it is realized that more red squirrels exist per square mile in the spruce-balsam forests of the Adirondacks than any other area in the state. And their numbers do not diminish.

The situation is not new.

In 1918 Edward W. Nelson, Chief, United States Biological Survey, who spent his early boyhood in the Adirondacks, said:

"Practically all species of northern warblers, vireos (small, singing, insect-eating birds), thrushes, chickadees, nuthatches and others are numbered among their victims. The notable scarcity of birds in northern forests may be largely due to these handsome but vicious marauders."

Nelson was writing for the National Geographic Magazine.

He also stated:

"The worst trait and one which largely overbalances all his many attractive qualities is his thoroughly proved habit of eating the eggs and young of small birds. During his breeding season he spends a large part of his time in predatory nest hunting, and the number of useful and beautiful birds he thus destroys must be almost incalculable."

Most assuredly the red is noticeable for far more than his reputation as a hit-squirrel, guilty of mass bird murder. He is easily recognizable by his rusty red coat, his incessant chatter, his frenzied movements, his constant hyperactivity.

Clayt Seagears, former Director of the Division of Conservation Education in the old New York State Conservation Department, calls the animal "Twitch-Pants."

Said Seagears in an issue of The Conservationist Magazine:

"When Twitch has an audience it is not possible for him to climb down a tree, normally considered a simple operation for a squirrel, without burning sufficient energy to last a turtle a lifetime.

"A reasonably tight hide is the only separation between the squirrel and an explosion, for Nature has certainly endowed him with a perpetual hot-foot. Even when standing still, which is extremely seldom, this small disciple of St. Vitus gives the impression that many watch springs are going off simultaneously inside."

If the red is vicious insofar as birds are concerned, it evidences equal ferocity toward its own kind. Fights between males during spring are wild and horrific tangles. As one observer puts it:

"I have seen the victim go up and down tree after tree, shrieking in fear and agony and leaving a trail of blood on the snow as he tried to escape his truculent pursuer."

Even the larger gray squirrel is not immune. They are not killed by the reds with ease, but they are killed.

In habitat the red shows a decided preference for coniferous forests, of pine, fir, spruce, balsam and hemlock. But conifers lacking, Mr. Chatterbox is adaptable to hardwood stands. His will, for instance, include beechnuts as part of food stored.

Which leads into the question: Has this small beast, considered "cute" by many vacationists who know not of his habits, offered any benefit of any kind to the world in which it lives?

In fairness it can be said that the red stores great quantities of pine, spruce, and other cones, sometimes in large, sheltered heaps — literally bushels of them. Many times the seeds are also buried, thus adding to forest growth.

The state conservation department has, on occasion, raided seed stores without benefit of a search warrant for nursery stocks. The same holds true in the West, where Man adds to his supply of pine cones. Such contributions, however, hardly balance the murderous instincts so readily displayed in blotting out bird life.

If Mr. Chatterbox is agile in trees, from which outposts they bark, scold and chatter when startled, almost, it seems, in a frenzy, the rodent is also an excellent swimmer.

When new food sources are sought, they will voluntarily swim the width of Lake George and Lake Champlain — at the widest points. Water holds no terror.

Home pads are nests, built of twigs, leaves and grasses, lined with soft materials such as fibrous barks. They are built in tree cavities or on limbs near the trunk. They also have been found in the ground, under roots or in brush heaps.

The young are produced usually around May, each weighing less than an ounce, each quite naked and totally helpless. Seagears points out they are born even without ear holes. The gestation period is about forty days.

When late June rolls around, they're pretty much on their own and producing their own individual brand of woodland terror. Production rate continues high; usually in July the mother will bring another batch forth, containing from four to six of the little hellions, each awaiting its turn to assault Man's feathered friends.

It is interesting to note that in such destruction, only two forms of bird life are immune, the hawks and the owls.

The reason is quite simple; any member of the Forest Mafia would be crazy to seek out the young of parents who would, in an instance of violence, place the squirrel where many believe he should be placed — in the non sanctuary known as the stomach.

The Pileated Woodpecker

Woody, the pileated woodpecker rescued by Joseph Okoniewski, assistant to Dr. Stone after it was hit by a car, spent his convalescence at Delmar eating high off the hog. The bird was fed bits of venison from carcasses brought to the wildlife center for examination, as well as hardboiled eggs and dog foods. While it ate venison offered at the end of tweezers, a more natural setting was devised, specifically, a portion of a tree trunk, with holes bored into it. The goodies were thereupon stuffed into the holes and Woody got the idea he was back on his own. He was released after slight damage to his eye was healed.

It was a period of growing silence in both the forest and in the fields. The year was 1886. And for two days Dr. Frank Chapman of New York City became an observer of decorative feathers on the hats of women he saw on city streets.

The hats were worn proudly but they represented death.

In one afternoon Dr. Chapman observed seven hundred hats, and of this number, five hundred and forty-two were decorated with feathers, including those from thrushes, tanagers, swallows, robins, warblers, waxwings, bobolinks, larks, doves, orioles and even woodpeckers!

At least 40 species were noted in his survey.

There were no laws to protect the birds. Even the turkey buzzard was not immune. Little was done in the way of protection until after 1886 when the bird protection committee of the American Ornithologists Union drafted a bill to define, once and for all, game birds as compared to song and insectivorous birds and birds of plumage.

New York State adopted the law. But it was not until the Audubon Society began its campaign in 1909 that headway was made for national protection.

What happened was what could be expected during the period when song and insectivorous birds could be shot at will. Their populations diminished; not only were normal predators after them with teeth and claw, but Man, with gun and net.

Woody refused to perch on a finger or arm, preferring to do what comes naturally to a pileated, clinging to the trunk – in this case, the trunk of Dr. Ward Stone, state wildlife pathologist at the wildlife research center in Delmar.

66

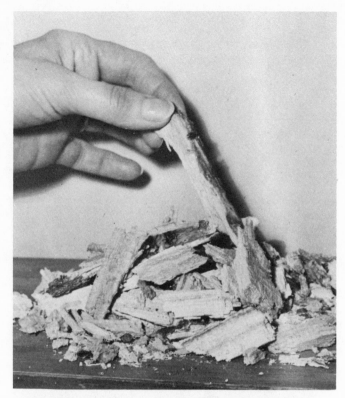

The chips hacked by a pileated woodpecker would put some beaver to shame. Admittedly the wood chipped is dead, but the size is extraordinary indeed.

A prime example of birdlife which fell prey to this outrageous killing for the sake of "beauty" was the pileated woodpecker, largest of all these novel birds which literally bore into trees for food. The pileated is a colorful creature, about the size of a crow, with a brilliant scarlet crest. It frequents hardwood and conifer forests. Its carpentry work is evidenced by a most unusual type of excavation, one which is large and almost rectangular in shape. The bird's power is such that it hammers out beaver-size chips. When it needs a nest in a dead tree it carves its own entrance and cavity. And, like all woodpeckers, it never gets a headache.

Not only human killers were to blame for the destruction of the pileated. The clearing of forestlands removed food sources and nesting sites.

The killing by Man has ceased, since the pileated, as are all woodpeckers, are now protected by both state and federal law, as are the owls and all species of hawks. The law also protects song birds, once killed not only for plumage, but actually for food. The New York State Department of Environmental Conservation today has, among its weapons against poachers, a German shepherd, trained to "sniff out" any such game shot by so-called "sportsmen." In too many cases, however, the slaughter continues.

There are still too many jackasses roaming the woods and fields with guns, ready to shoot almost anything that moves.

The pileated, also known as the "log cock" has also come under verbal fire because of its habit of attacking power or telephone poles, a move dimly viewed by utilities. It is not unusual for such poles to be damaged to such an extent that they must be replaced. The only time I ever saw a pileated droop in defeat was when it assaulted a pole and found it was made of metal. It probably retreated into the woodlands to wonder what God hath wrought!

An example of what carpenter ants, among favorite foods of the pileated, can do to a birch tree. The birch's outer surface appeared perfectly healthy, but the ants got into the interior and carved their familiar tunnels. The destructive insects will enter trees which have been "wounded" and will do a devastating job. In this instance, the birch, while giving the appearance of health, was toppled in a high wind.

This is what a carpenter ant looks like, magnified three times.

To kill a pileated is to kill a bird of enormous benefit. It is considered the greatest killer of carpenter ants and wood boring grubs. Reputedly it detects the presence of insects and grubs beneath what appears to be healthy bark by sound. The beak may be the instrument of destruction for bugs, but it also carries the sweet song of romance. The pileated also uses drumming in courtship.

Like many birds, birth and growth periods are not stretched out. Both parents share incubation and eggs are hatched in about 20 days. Less than 30 days later the young will be on their own developing their own menus.

Abandoned nests often are occupied by other birds or even mammals, including the flying squirrel. Natural enemies do not abound, but the pileated will, on occasion, fall prey to the peregrine falcon and the sharp-shinned hawk.

Once considered on the verge of extinction, the bird is back, still timid in the presence of Man, but still doing its wonderful job. It is back not only because of protection, but because the ravaging of forestlands has ceased and second and third growth timber has formed new habitat. The bird inhabits not only the Adirondacks, but to the joy of many, can be seen in municipal parklands.

Norway Rat

This rat, an inelegant beast, is most assuredly not a game animal, and is considered by many as the most destructive and hated of all mammals. While the skunk can be detested because of its artillery, that purveyor of obnoxious perfume is not repulsive.

The rat is.

The Norway travels under many aliases, including brown rat, house rat, barn rat and in some areas, as the water rat. It exists in fresh water as well as salt water areas. It exists in the Adirondack Park and its advent into the North Country, which once was free of rats, has contributed to several theories.

This rodent is thought to have expanded its habitat from Central Asia. It is believed to have invaded Europe in the early 1700's, when literally hordes of them swam the Volga River in Russia; Russia, obviously, imposed no travel restrictions in those days.

About 1730, the rat arrived in England aboard ships from the Orient. Once in England, it took over from the black rat, whose numbers decreased. And then on ships the browns crossed the Atlantic to the fertile shores of America.

How, finally, did it reach the Adirondacks?

There are two versions of interest.

De Kay, the naturalist, in the late 1800's, said:

"In this country it was introduced with the foreign mercenaries during the Revolutionary War. They (the rats) are now numerous in all the states and have even extended into Canada."

From the naturalist C. Hart Merriam:

"This ubiquitous naturalized exotic is found even within the confines of the Adirondacks. But his presence here omens no good. Like the lumberman, whose footsteps he follows, he is the personification of destruction and desecrates the soil on which he treads."

In the late 1800's the brown rat was found in certain areas of Essex County; its habitat included houses, outbuildings such as barns, and fields.

If indeed it came with mercenaries, this would mean it arrived with the Hessians, presumably in shipments made along with the hired German soldiers. Most assuredly they were not brought along as pets, despite the German love for animals, once they landed in America.

A second version was given by the late Archibald T. Shorey ("A.T." to his friends, of which I was one) who died in 1974, a few days before his 92nd birthday. Shorey was born in Bridgton, Maine, and knew the coastline well; eventually became a newspaperman in New York, and then joined the old New York State

The Norway rat is certainly not a "game" animal, but it does exist in the mountain areas. An import during the 1800's, it serves a purpose insofar as predators are concerned. Owls, hawks and mammalian carnivores consider the rodent part of their menus.

Conservation Department, where he became known as the "father" of the Adirondack trail system. His interest in the North Country was vast, dated far back; he became a member of the Adirondack Mountain Club, for instance, in 1923.

Shorey believed the rodents began their trek to the Adirondacks when ships in the China trade berthed at Bath, Maine, and deserted the vessels.

Their expansion in habitat was helped when they were carried in a big convoy of supplies from the coast, a convoy of beef-on-the-hoof, and grain for feeding. This convoy stopped in Keene for several days while en route to the army on the St. Lawrence River. This occurred during the War of 1812, between England and America.

Howsoever the rat came to the mountains is immaterial at this point; like the gypsy moth, it is here to stay and be endured. It poses little menace and while a pest, it has enemies other than Man. Owls and hawks for instance. Bobcats for another. One also can count coyotes and foxes among the mammals. The browns, like the bear, favor dumps which are not properly administered.

It is interesting to note that the brown rat apparently drove the black rat, another unwelcome visitor to the American shores, into oblivion; the brown is larger, more ferocious. The black rat was another immigrant from Europe during the Revolution.

The browns bear four to five times a year, with from four to ten in a litter. Fortunately not all survive. They will kill nesting birds as well as poultry; feed on crops and stored grains and, reportedly, are to be noted in areas where food supplies are constant.

What you see was once real-life; events changed radically for the fisher, however, since the figure is a mounting. Trophy is at Marty's Tavern, Indian Lake, run by Walter Harr; the well-known tavern is part of a motel and liquor store complex. The business was formerly operated by Marty Harr, who moved to Indian Lake from Schenectady, where he was employed in the old Hotel Van Curler.

The Fisher

Consider, if you will, a most unusual mammal, a member of the weasel family, called the fisher or the black cat, pekan, Pennant's marten or pekan cat.

It received no protection in New York State until 1937 when the State Legislature decreed a closed season for an indefinite period.

That period ended in 1950 when trappers were allowed an open season, the first in thirteen years.

What makes the animal unusual is that despite its size — it is one of the larger members of the weasel group — it is not only an expert swimmer, but is of such agility in trees that it can outspeed and catch a squirrel as part of its menu.

It also represents death to the porcupine, a less than attractive rodent whose skills at destroying valuable trees by girdling hikes the blood pressure of any forester or forestland owner who values such growth.

To devour this animated mass of barbed quills, or more specifically, the meat underneath, the fisher will go for the belly, which is free from spikes. From then on, once proper assassination has been completed, the fisher will eat the porcupine "from the inside out."

It does not always kill with impunity. When quills are ingested with flesh, the spines align themselves in bundles in the intestines and pass through, a most remarkable procedure. Not all follow such a route, however. Fisher pelts often disclose quills which have traveled into areas just under the skin from parts distant.

The fisher is of suitable size for its accomplishments. A male can measure about a yard in length and weigh in the neighborhood of nine pounds or a bit more. Hunters have sometimes killed them by mistake, thinking they were shooting at a fox. In the dimness of twilight, some observers have sworn they have seen an "immature black panther." Such is the magnification not only of twilight but imagination. Fishermen experience the same delight.

Porcupines do not furnish the only source of protein. The fisher will eat squirrels, hares, cottontails, nesting birds, mice, rats and fish. The beast has been known to feast upon deer carcasses, the result of a whitetail dying a lonely death, far from the hunter who shot it, or a whitetail which succumbed to winter's deadly chill and starvation. Even though the fisher is a member of the weasel family, it does not possess the utter ferocity of the smaller, common weasel; oddly enough, the ferocity of these mammals apparently increases in proportion to decrease in size.

Other than a furbearer, the black cat is useful to Man in that every porcupine it kills means less trees are mutilated and die.

An interesting point in the history of the fisher: The demonstration of how Man can devastate a species if law does not hold the hunter in check. The black cat is back in the Adirondacks in volume, but this was not always the case. Before protection was offered, the animal could be taken in any manner, day or night, and those seeking its fur made every effort to take only the young or the female since their fur was of more value than old males.

During winter when fisher tracks materialized on the forest floor, they were followed to the burrow or to a tree. Traps were set in some instances. The tree was felled in others; the kill made by gun.

Such killing had the usual dismal effect; the population went down. At one time, the black cat was thought to have been exterminated. But a few wary ones remained. And by 1940 or thereabouts, numbers were on the increase.

Game researchers now say the Adirondack population may equal, if not surpass, the numbers which existed when the mountains were virgin, which once they were indeed.

Mr. Untouchable

Originator of the art of acupuncture, but not for healing — that's the porcupine, pictured in this drawing by Clayt Seagears, which appeared in The Conservationist Magazine. It is not the most hospitable of creatures as any of its colleagues in the wild will attest, since its barbed quills can cause a slow death.

Let's start with a quotation, to wit:

"The porcupine is our forest's best example of the intellectual degeneration that comes to those who possess what seems to be an invincible defense."

The quote is from the late Dave Cook, Albany, retired conservation department forester.

I doubt if anyone could have put it better.

The porcupine is an animal that bewilders, fascinates and arouses ribald curiosity, particularly in connection with its romancing period during the mating season which, one might add, fortunately produces only one young a year.

If one considers this novel animal as one which does not draw interest, the old Saturday Evening Post can set him straight. A full page ad, appearing in that magazine many years ago, displayed a mother porcupine crossing a log, followed by four or five prickly sprouts. The magazine promptly received and made mention of, a large volume of letters pointing to the error.

One young is enough, despite the fact that the loner is born with soft bristles which harden in a short time. And they remain hard. Ribaldry enters the picture when discussion centers upon the physical act of mating. It is sufficient to say both male and female cooperate without disastrous results.

As the full grown animal ambles amiably through the quiet of the woods, it sounds as though someone is dragging a sackful of potato chips; the porky is a grunter, growler, a waddler with the grace of a duck wearing a hernia truss. It climbs a tree with the concentrated deliberation of a drunk threading a needle and some will swear that a young one will pass through puberty, adolescence and attain senility by the time it reaches anywhere near the top. Mr. Untouchable is not exactly a sprinter of Olympic caliber.

If there were an Adirondack award for a flag pole endurance sitting contest, the porky would win it paws down. Often it climbs a tree, settles in a comfortable crotch and spends a day or more contentedly gnawing bark and in so doing, often the tree is killed by girdling. Its favorites seem to be larch or Scotch pine but it is not too particular. In winter, when the animal is in its den area, it will go after hardwood bark at the tree's base.

In proportion to its size, (one may reasonably compare a fat cocker spaniel), the porcupine is as heavily armored as the Civil War's Monitor and its defense is a dense coat of barbed spines so thick and sharp that a fair sized flea would be impaled if the bug were mentally retarded enough to try penetration. It has the intelligence of a mongoloid turtle, a thick skull to match, massive muscles for one so small and, being a rodent, it possesses large gnawing teeth.

Head-on, it has the vacant look of a sleep walker. Its stomach is more than amply equipped for the herbs, twigs and leaves it receives, and it is a nut-gone-loose on any salt impregnated object.

No sportsman's latrine, temporary or otherwise, however staunchly built or protected, is safe from the porky's teeth or appetite; furniture touched by the sweat of Man will be chewed energetically and many a camper has lost both paddle and temper because of the quill-pig's chomping. Sweat stained tools, such as axe handles, for instance, constitute the cream on the pie.

The late Conservation Officer Chester Griffith of Schenectady, once showed this writer a piece of aluminum from an airplane which crashed in the Adirondacks. It had been chewed. Deer antlers, dropped to the forest floor following the end of their usefulness – usually over a four-month period from December through March – vanish not only from the desire of a field mouse for calcium, but from a porcupine's as well.

Like the skunk, an animal without armor and at times without honor, the porky moves with notable serenity and calmness. When annoyed by an animal afflicted with temporary insanity, such as a dog or coyote, its defense mechanism functions with astonishing rapidity.

Its head goes down, its rear legs pull into a crouch and nothing is offered save the thick underbrush of spikes and agony. Thus it protects its belly, the most vulnerable spot and the one usually sought by any carnivore such as the fisher or bear interested in curtailing its future.

The tail can be manipulated with extraordinary speed and it is this maneuver which has given rise to the myth that the animal can propel its barbed spears with a bowman's ability. But this is pure myth; the quills (between 20,000 to 30,000 over the entire body area) are easily detachable and once anchored in the opposition, remain; the barbed spikes work inward and in many cases, cause slow death. Ernest Thompson Seton the naturlist once described the porcupine as the "Knight of many spears." An apt description.

An eagle, examined days after an encounter with the porcupine, died of starvation because quills were set in its throat. The writer's dog tangled with Mr. Untouchable on an Adirondack trip and thereby learned 200 good reasons why the name is applied; that many spears were extracted from mouth and jaws.

The porky is not protected by law, is considered by foresters and woodlot owners as a destroyer. Many individuals who travel the woodlands will shoot the animal on sight.

Like the woodchuck, teeth continue to grow and a porcupine without trees to wear them down would end as a porcupine with teeth passing downward and upward through its skull. Thus the animal attains a status peculiar to few others –– it can commit suicide with its own incisors.

For many years but not too much in the present, the protection of the animal has been advocated by some on the basis that a "lost" hunter or other person can kill them with a club and thus survive on their flesh until help arrives.

Actually, manners of preparation do exist for brewing up a portion of porky. In roasting the beast, meat can be cooked over a open fire, or if it is a young quill-pig, it can be spitted. In building up a stew, one might parboil the meat in salted water and with suitable additions, continuing the preparation over an open fire.

"Lost" persons, however, usually lack proper utensils and staples for such a meal and are under additional handicaps. The animal is not easy to locate at a moment's notice; killing them with a club is a bit on the gruesome side, and unless the individual possesses a sharp skinning knife and matches, he must eat the flesh raw. Faced by that ordeal, hope may vanish.

Once quilled, a suffering animal needs prompt attention. In the instance of a pet, the spines must be pulled straight out with a quick jerk; pliers or tweezers will do the job. Wounds thus created may be treated as other puncture ones.

The spines are modified hairs. Nature enlarged them, made them hollow, smooth, and affixed the broadheads. No one has seen a porky completely denuded of spears for a simple reason. They are replaced.

As a "menace" to humanity, the quill-pig never will attain professional football status. Mr. Untouchable's low birth rate is one factor against tribal increase. Routine killing by humans is another. And, of course, Man's contributions to partial extermination of many species –– the modern automobile –– kills hundreds annually.

One might thus include the automobile as a comparatively new predator in the Adirondack scene, a mechanical monster not yet quite up to the estimated 520-horsepower evidenced by the powerful Blue whale, but with a robotish lack of discrimination in its murderous onslaughts.

72

Mr. Stub Tail

View of a bay lynx, or bobcat, in complacent mood. This one is held in captivity, appears in good shape.

About five years ago one sunny midday while walking the railroad tracks southward from Rt. 28N, there occurred what I consider a most unusual incident.

Ahead of me was my dog, busily investigating everything under the bright sun — except an animal which had quietly emerged from heavy underbrush about fifty feet ahead of her nose.

The animal proceeded southward, joining our caravan, but instead of using the railroad bed of stone and ties, walked skillfully on one of the tracks.

There is no understanding to this day why the dog did not notice its presence until a half minute passed. And when she did, the greyhound in her went into action; she was off in foolish pursuit like a rocket.

Ensued a most remarkable scene. The dog was almost upon the animal when the latter sensed her presence, turned, leaped into the air and came down running. It disappeared into nearby growth with nary a sound. The dog, startled, skidded to stop, idiotic wonderment on its face.

It was lucky she didn't overtake the animal.

It was a bobcat, Lynx rufus in academic circles, otherwise known as the bay lynx or wildcat.

* * * * * *

It was not the first sighting for this writer of the bobcat in the wild, but I remain puzzled over the fact that this shy and retiring mammal, so sensitive to its surroundings, failed to note not only the dog but the human behind it. I do realize one indisputable fact; had the dog made contact, all hell would have broken loose. The cat is a savage fighter and has weapons to match its ferocity, in the form of sharp teeth and pin-sharp claws.

Lynx rufus is no stranger to the Adirondacks despite heavy hunting pressures of the past. It is not considered an endangered or threatened species in the state itself. It rules its territorial domain in the North Country in fairly good numbers, probably more so than in the Catskills, where it is common.

DRAWN
FROM MALE
IN TAWNY
SUMMER COAT

In these excellent drawings by Clayt Sea-gears, the bobcat is presented in two aspects, its "fighting face," and its hunger leap. Drawing at right shows a bobcat in the process of obtaining a meal of ordinary house cat. The art work appeared in The Conservationist Magazine.

It has held firm to the Adirondacks. At the turn of the century this finely formed, graceful animal was considered exterminated from the state except for portions in the hill country, the Catskills and the Hudson highlands. At one time bounties were placed on it. That, of course, is a thing of the past, and wisely so, since the cat fills its own niche in the scheme of things.

It may kill deer, but the deer are small or weakened. It subsists upon smaller animals, including the cottontail, rodents and birds. It may, on occasion, seek a beaver — or, in the vicinity of a settled area, the common housecat. Hunger draws no distinction between a wild or domesticated animal if, indeed, a housecat roaming the woods can be called domesticated.

Adults may range from fifteen to thirty pounds; ferocity and ability to exist remain constant.

Like any member of the cat family the bobcat is an excellent stalker, of great patience, a tree climber of ability, and an excellent swimmer if the need arises. Two to four young are born in the spring, remain with Mama until fall when, having been taught appropriate methods of hunting, they are off on their own.

Seldom seen during daylight, they are, in the main, nocturnal; once seen, they are unforgettable in their color, described as "spotted, rusty-gray." There is resemblance to the Canada lynx — which may exist in the deep wilderness areas of the Adirondacks. But the lynx is a larger animal, lighter in color, and has more pronounced chin whiskers as well as highly visible ear tufts. A look at the short and stubby tail will differentiate the two easily.

The bobcat has only a black patch on the top of that appendage, while the lynx has a black band of fur completely encircling it. The question of why the bobcat and the lynx possess only short tails, while other members of the cat family own longer such appurtenances, has never been answered. Perhaps there may be legend connected to the story. Who knows? It is not important anyway; it bothers not the bobcat or lynx.

Interesting to note is that the cat, like the fisher, will assault a porcupine when he is hungry. The cat, however, is not always as fortunate as the fisher, because there have been instances noted where quills have worked into the area of the mouth to such an extent, eating became painful, and starvation set in.

As long as dense spruce swamps, as long as the forest remains in the Adirondacks, the bobcat will be with us, voicing his lonely cry, which once heard, remains in memory. As one observer once put it.:

"The squall, while frightening to some, is no different from the tomcat perched on your back fence. If there is a difference, it is in the fact that the volume has been turned up!"

Photo represents a near tragedy for this bobcat. Animal was caught in a trap (left rear leg) but it did not meet with death; it was released.

Newcomer

The original "bag man" of the forest — the opossum, a marsupial with unusual baby care arrangement; Mama carries her young in a pouch on her belly. The animal is fairly common; is a fierce fighter when its life is threatened.

At the century's turn the only animal in New York State that carries its young in what might be called a personalized, attached shopping bag, was considered a "recent species."

The meaning is clear. The animal, the opossum, had begun its northward move into the state and was beginning to be noticed.

Its invasion of the state had occurred for some time. In February, 1899, the Buffalo Express made note that "a possum had been shot at Hamburg, Erie County," and the item contained this line:

"It is the first animal of the specie (sic) shot in this vicinity in 25 years."

Which, of course, would place the marsupial in the state during the mid 1870's. Erie County is in western New York. Opossums were also reported in the southern counties of the state, as well as in Long Island. Conclusion: The peculiar looking little rascals were migrating from Pennsylvania.

Whatever their migratory habits, the animals fascinate students of wildlife.

They have extended their range into the Adirondacks.

They are here to stay and hunting and trapping pressures won't bother them since their hide is tender, worth little. A coat of 'possum fur hasn't, as yet, the status symbol of mink. Furthermore, while the flesh is eaten by financially strapped southerners, in whose domain the beast abounds, it is certainly not considered a delicacy in the north.

I quote a description given by Dr. William J. Hamilton Jr., Cornell University:

"If parboiled for three hours, the body cavity filled with onions and garlic, placed on a thin oak plank, laced with bacon and broiled for a full afternoon, one will find the plank fairly edible!"

On a non-gastronomical note, Paul M. Kelsey of EnCon, a noted writer on the world of animals, says:

"The stereotype 'possum of children's story books or the comics is usually seen hanging by its tail from a branch. They can, but they usually don't. With their prehensile tail and opposable thumb on their hind foot, they are very adept at climbing, enabling them to get fruit and occasionally escape predators. They are much more at home on the ground, and given their 'druthers, will dive into a woodchuck hole or similar ground cavity, rather than climb a tree."

Kelsey also points out they are seldom bothered by mammalian carnivores and taken occasionally by the great horned owl. One can believe that. The great horned is not the world's greatest epicure. It also eats skunks.

Another predator is the iron carnivore known as the automobile; many drivers who see carcasses on concrete or blacktop mistake them for giant rats. There is a resemblance.

I would consider the most interesting aspect of this creature as its process of birth and early growth. Its reproductive rate, incidentally, is high.

Hard to believe, but the young come into this harsh world about the size of a honeybee and are born in less than thirteen days. The mites join the rank of the living with well developed front legs, but they are considered little more than rudimentary fetuses!

The front legs work, however, and the young pull themselves slowly a few inches up the mother's belly to the pouch, their future home for the next month-and-one-half or two. Mama helps them in their hike by moistening a pathway through her fur. Once inside the warm and dark cavern, the young find an odd number of nipples, thirteen, to be exact.

Here Nature grows wicked and can be accused of child abuse.

The nipples, and, therefore, the live-giving food, are available only on a first-come, first-served basis. Once a youngster attaches himself to a spigot, he reamins attached.

Latecomers starve.

When the nipple days are over the young fortunate enough to survive emerge from the sanctuary and ride the mother's back, clinging to fur. They do not ride suspended from an upbended tail, as some think. A few weeks later they depart to face the world alone. At this point they are about the size of a small rat.

Food? Like the bear, the opossum will eat almost everything. Fruit is a much sought after item. To add to its menu the animal will consume insects, carrion, worms, small snakes, bird eggs, meadow mice, slugs, grain, frogs and in human settlement areas, ripe garbage.

Hardly a gourmet, the possum will also eat toads and this is a remarkable feat because most carnivores avoid these garden hoppers because of the toxic secretions in a toad's glands. Ever watched your dog grab a toad in its mouth, suddenly look stricken, and drop it suddenly with a look of disgust?

If an accusing finger can be pointed at the animal, it would be because of its habit of destroying eggs in ground nesting birds. But that infuriating fact to bird lovers can be balanced off by the knowledge that the same animal destroys agricultural pests.

The phrase "playing possum" is a familiar one.

It has basis in fact. When faced with an enemy, the opossum' sometimes will play a death scene but this is considered an involuntary reaction rather than a carefully thought-out tactic. (Playing death to an animal which wants not only to kill but devour would hardly serve as a deterrent).

Most assuredly the action is not one of cowardice since the opossum is a fierce fighter when need arises. Most of the time when it faces danger it will attempt to escape. It is not gifted with speed, however, and its dash for safety is described as a "waddle."

If the animal has the attributes of a kangaroo in that it keeps its young pouch-ridden, it also possesses one of the attributes of an elephant. Only in this case, it is the tail, not the trunk. The tail is prehensile, that is, the appendage is able to seize or grasp. And the opossum uses it in many ways. One is to carry bedding into its den; the procedure is worthy of note; dry leaves and grasses are gathered first with the mouth, then passed under the belly with its front feet, where the material is neatly wrapped by the tail for transport.

As for intellect, it possesses little. I think Kelsey's comment is revealing. That gentleman said:

"As proof that its survival can't be credited to wit, a physical examination is revealing. To compare the brain sizes of a 'possum and a raccoon, beans were placed in the brain cavity of skulls of comparably sized animals.

"The 'possum skull held 25, while the raccoon held 150!"

The Panther

In Lake George's simpler days when the term water skiers referred to insects rather than curvaceous Dianas and spindle-legged teen-agers whose midriffs are blown to balloon proportions by inflated life preservers, there was an Indian named Sampson Paul.

One day Sampson allowed he'd do some fish spearing. This was permissable in the days of this Abenaki, for the soft bite of the canoe paddle had not yet been interrupted by the raucous roars of outboards and inboards, lake trout swam the shallow bays fearlessly, and state law had not yet gotten around to viewing spearing as a feat to be squelched.

With pronged spear, Paul left his home on Diamond Island in early morning, as the mist still clung to the lake, and boated toward the mainland shore — and while enroute almost died before his time.

Swimming near him of a sudden was a huge mountain lion, or panther, its head held high as cats will do in the water, its muscular legs propelling it forward in lunges. Sampson was not one to avoid a clash; he drove his spear deep into the animal. As one might expect, that particular beast became extinct and the subject of an obituary.

The lean and tawny panther, also known as the cougar, puma, mountain lion or "painter," was not unknown in the Adirondacks. As pointed out in Volume 1 of Adirondack Album, it was an object much sought by bounty hunters, and in the late 1800's the top bounty hunter of all, George Muir, from Harrisville, (northwestern Adirondacks) managed to blow away sixty-seven for a bounty of $20 each.

This powerful animal is oft mentioned in diaries of fighters in the unit known as Rogers Rangers. On one scout in the Lake George region, for instance, when the Rangers were returning from the Ticonderoga area in the mid 1700's, they ran across a panther living out its life in sorrowful fashion; it was toothless, infirm and starving, and was killed on the winter's ice sheath as a matter of course.

In those early days the puma prowled not only the North Country but the entire United States, and it can still be found in some portions of the U.S., in Canada, as well as in Central America and South America.

It is an animal whose present-day existence is open to question in the Adirondacks. There are those who say the panther is indeed an inhabitant, and there are others who deride the opinion. The late Perry Ehlers, who ran a small outdoor equipment store perched on the banks of the Hudson River at North River, told us he not only had seen tracks, but the animal itself.

My notes of years ago mention that the Wells family of Schenectady on June 30, 1951, while traveling to camp on Auger Lake in Essex County, near Keeseville, at 12:45 a.m., spotted an animal about six feet long, about two-and-one half feet high, and tawny in color.

Mr. Wells, in his recount to state officials, said he wasn't "trying to sell anyone a bill of goods," but both he and another member of his family "know what we saw."

There was Earl F. Crombach, Ontario, who hunted Franklin County, who reported a panther sighting and who said: "I have no doubt that panthers have come back in New York State."

A member of the Todd family, Edwards, St. Lawrence County, went back in time, reported that about 1905 his mother was followed by a panther. G.W. MacLaughlin, an executive at Camillus High School, told state officials in 1951 (a year of panther reports, it seems) that about 1920, while hunting with Frank Bergeron, Burlington, Vt., in the Rogers Rock area, south of Ticonderoga, that Bergeron had spotted an animal which he later identified from a book photo as a panther.

Additional reports came from the Pharoah mountain area, which is between Schroon Lake and Ticonderoga, Essex County.

All these incidents might well be true; who would doubt the opinions of several? The author himself saw plaster casts made of a track located in Saratoga County in the 1950's and the track was later identified by a state zoologist as one made by a panther.

Bill Roden, noted outdoor columnist and former president of the New York State Conservation Council, an Adirondacker well versed in things wild and unusual, in 1975 reported a highway crew in Franklin County had, a few years previously, seen a panther cross a road in front of a highway truck in early morning.

In 1973, said Roden, a Chestertown couple reported sighting one of the big cats at their camp; plaster casts were made, and experts identified them as cat tracks with the mountain lion as a "possible maker."

During the same period there were reports of sightings in the West Mountain area of Warren County.

In his special wildlife report for the Temporary Study Commission on the Future of the Adirondacks, made a short time before the creation of the Adirondack Park Agency. Dr. C.H.D. Clarke discussed the reports of sightings in the eastern United States, including the Adirondacks, and concluded:

"Maintenance of populations at low densities must mean that individual ranges are enormous. If the animal seen today were here tomorrow and the next day he would soon be killed. Denning females must be very secretive. There is no predicting what would happen if panthers were released. Under the circumstances, one can state that there is as much hope of eastern panthers establishing themselves in the Adirondacks as there is of getting stock to release."

Not all panthers killed in the late 1800's were shot for bounties. A two-hundred pounder was killed by Verplanck Colvin, who served as superintendent of survey for the state, in Hamilton County. Colvin's catch apparently was one of a pair that made a 30-mile circuit in the area, according to L.H. Gillies, father of William (Bill) Gillies, Colvin's guide. Gillies, who moved to North Carolina, recalled that Rube Carey killed a young panther somewhere near Raquette Lake and it was mounted and displayed at a bar at Long Lake for a spell, undoubtedly sparking off many a tall tale.

Toward the last of its hey-day, it was an oddity of fact that the bounty placed upon this big cat was less than that placed on the timber wolf, which was worth $30 a head. The panther's price, as noted, was $20 a head, equally dead. Also unusual was that the powerful Iroquois viewed the panther in a lesser light.

Iroquoian clans who hunted the Adirondacks were symbolized by animals, including the wolf, bear and the turtle. The puma was conspicuously absent.

Which is strange indeed, because it was the Indians of the state who introduced the animal to early white settlers of New York, who thought the beast was really a lion of African variety. Vanderock's History relates that "although the New Netherlands lie in a fierce climate and the country in winter seems rather cold, nevertheless lions are found there, but not by the Christians!"

This novel statement was explained by Hugh Fosburgh, author of "The Natural Thing," in this fashion:

"They were found by the Indians who brought the skins into the settlements. The thing that troubled the New Netherlanders was that none of the skins had the manes that they associated with male lions; they therefore concluded they were all females and went on to do some nice biological invention to account or this."

Why was the panther so ceaselessly sought?

There are no records of man-eaters and the animal today in its western strongholds, avoids humans. The reason, or at least one of them, is simple; humans resented the predator's attack not only on domestic stock, but upon deer. It was estimated that a mature panther could well devour one deer a week. There were those who said there was plenty of evidence that the animal killed a good deal more than it could consume.

Using this figure it becomes apparent that one hundred panthers could kill and assimilate into muscle and sinew, more than 5,000 deer a year. This was just too much for sportsmen of that long ago age to take. They preferred to kill the white-tail by jacklighting, running by dogs, or leisurely killing from a boat after the white-tail had been hounded into a lake or pond. The idea of allowing the panther — or the timber wolf — to cut into the deer herd was an absurdity unthinkable, particularly with the deer herd itself diminishing under the murderous "solicitude" of Man.

The question of current existence, therefore, seems to be arguable. But once again, the thought: Isn't it possible for an animal, once shot out of existence, to return to haunts which once held its spoor?

It is a thought upon which to ponder, since once again the phrase comes to mind, to wit: Nothing in Nature remains static.

Above: Panther sculpture by Marchand, as displayed in the old New York State Museum many years ago. Below: The real thing, a captive, half-trained panther (or puma) gazes steadfastly at the camera in the pose reminiscent of a hard-hearted capitalist studying a recently bereaved widow asking for a loan.

Mr. Cheeks - Lovable Nuisance

What happens, pray tell, when a chipmunk gets tired of eating peanuts while perched on a stump or log? A simple question, with a simple answer: He "takes to the road" in his private chipmunkmobile. For proof, see above. This novel photo was snapped by Alice Clements of Philadelphia while vacationing in the Adirondacks.

I don't know if you have noticed the enigma presented by that delightful nuisance, the chipmunk, but any farm, any summer camp or cottage will offer the puzzle.

The chipmunk is a burrower; the entrance to its den may lead to an extensive series of tunnels, some twenty or more feet in length; the entrance is often within a few feet of the exit, and within the subterranean highways there exist the den and storage cavities, the former lined with leaves. Into this underground pantry go nuts and seeds and anything else edible — a storehouse for the days when cold weather closes in and the chippie decides to forsake more enjoyable days above ground.

The enigma?

Both entrance and exit to this underground labrinth are clean; that is, there is no piled dirt. Yet in the excavation of not only tunnels but nesting and storage chambers, literally pounds of dirt must be removed and disposed of.

How does the chippie, which is a form of ground squirrel, dispose of the excavated dirt?

Very few explanations are offered. One version is that the dirt is carried off, leaving the entrance, for instance, with the appearance of a neatly drilled hole in the ground. Another is that the loose dirt is thrown out through another hole at some distance from the digging, and dispersed and that this disposal cavity is then kept plugged with earth.

Whatever, it remains an interesting question.

And the tiny rodent, marked by five dark stripes and two white stripes on its back, remains an interesting animal.

For one thing, there are the cheek pouches. Feed a chipmunk sunflower seeds and watch what happens. The seeds are not immediately devoured, but go into pouches and as each seed finds it way into the collection, the pouches grow in size, until by comparison, the area of the head grows in size to a ridiculous degree. Once filled, the animal will dash to the entrance of its den, there to add to growing stores of food.

On its way to its pantry, it may pass another chamber which is used as a sanitary facility!

While most associate the chipmunk as an eater of seeds, the variety of food sought is incredible. Wheat is devoured, so is corn. Grass seed, ragweed seed, acorns, beechnuts, strawberries, blueberries, wintergreen berries and even mushrooms are eaten.

Surprisingly, this two to three ounce creature will, on occasion, eat snails, beetles, insect larvae, frogs, salamanders, young birds and eggs. Most astonishing, however, is that while large snakes constitute a predator, they will eat small ones!

The major enemies include not only snakes but cats, foxes, martens and birds of prey, such as the hawk. One cannot forget the weasel, the terror of their existence; the weasel is a horror of major importance, because it is slim enough, ferocious enough, to enter burrows and to kill underground. There is no escape from this ruthless animal.

The chippies live in lowlands and highlands, including mountain tops. They exist even on Mount Washington in New Hampshire, where world record wind velocities have been recorded.

They are expert climbers and when startled will often take to the heights, "chucking" warnings for all to heart. During any dash for safety their running posture might be considered absurd; their tail is held erect and at times will quiver noticeably.

They are hibernators but rarely spend more than five months in sleep. Much depends upon the weather topside. If a warm period ensues, they may awaken and prowl a bit, but cold weather will send them back into their snug nests. Generally by the middle of March, the males are above ground, searching for conquests. Usually they have found agreeable females by April, and the females will give birth in about a month to from three to five chipmunklings, if the word may be used.

It takes only another month for the youngsters to greet the world and the food it holds above ground. And then, if near human habitation, such as summer camps, the fun begins. The young will play, chasing one another. The adults will pursue food sources, which in many cases are campers who offer handouts. A small degree of patience will diminish their natural wariness and many a vacationer has returned to city homes, ecstatic over the fact that he or she has "tamed" the tiny creatures to eat out of the human hand. They are persistent. And many summer cottage owners have found a door left even partially open is an invitation to a kitchen guest.

They are lovable creatures, clean in habit, delightful to the eye, quick in movements, ever watchful, an animal which has accustomed itself to the intruder known as Man.

Long may the rascal exist; its damage is negligable; its worth to the human vast in enjoyment. There are times when I think God must have created the chippie because He felt that the land needed a perky, industrious and lively creature to enliven Man's existence, to teach him that kindness can be repaid in total delight.

The Great Unloved

It's an old joke, but bears repeating: Victims of the above animal often have threatened to have it arrested on a charge of fragrancy. Not too unusual if you consider the odor emitted by a skunk as an unusual woodland perfume!

Nobody knows when ancient man first came into contact with Mephitis mephitis, but it must have been a moment of horrendous proportions and if the gentleman had a spouse, she must have hung him on a rawhide clothesline outside the family cave for several days.

She would have had good reason, since Mephitis mephitis is the academic way of referring to an animal well known for its artillery and marksmanship, the common or striped skunk.

The Carthaginian general Hannibal who crossed the Alps with elephants to attack Roman legions might well have succeeded in defeating them if he had substituted Mephitis mephitis for the pachyderms. Napoleon might never have spent his final and gloomy days on an island if he had brought the little animals instead of soldiers into the Battle of Waterloo. And one wonders what might have happened if Gen. Burgoyne, instead of buttressing his invading army with Hessians, had marched with 5,000 skunks into the Battle of Saratoga.

The skunk, valuable for its fur and sometimes for its meat, is the inventor of fluid nerve gas. Nobody in his right mind would dispute the patent which, of course, this amiable waddler of forest and field has never filed.

As a marksman, the skunk is a trick shot artist; using no mirror, he fires from the rear and observes the consequences by a look over his shoulder. The reason for this is that he possesses his "scent" glands or sacs in the rear of his anatomy and powerful pressures from gripping thighs can send the spray to ten feet or more.

Skunks often meet people, since they like to roam where people roam — and live. Most of the time the meeting has no consequence, unless the human presents a problem. In which case the animal gives warning; the bushy tail is hiked to clear the deck for action. If annoyance persists, the animal goes into action and the result is total envelopment in an odor remininscent of exploding gas bubbles from a swamp enjoying its decaying process.

Suggested remedies to cure the results of an encounter are numerous, but the most positive remedy is a simple one: Remain a suitable distance from the creature, even though it is slow to arouse, and in many instances, can be made into a gentle pet.

Fortunate is the person who inadvertently stumbles upon one of these beasts and lives to tell the tale in polite company shortly thereafter. It happened to me just once — this close encounter — and by extraordinary good fortune the skunk apparently realized I was no threat. He must have seen, even in the darkness, the look of shock on my face.

If one says all the world is against Mr. Untouchable, that isn't quite accurate. The world respects him, with certain exceptions. Skunk meat is part of the menu for the great horned owl, the wolf, coyote, foxes and badgers and the bobcat, all of whom seem not to be dismayed by what happens when a skunk fears for life.

The animal is one which has grown accustomed to Man; will live in close proximity, such as under porches, in garages and in outbuildings. Removing them is a major problem and, understandably, specialists in the business are few. I have seen biologists lift skunks by their tails and have been told that this is a safe method, since once their rear legs are disconnected from the firmness of the ground, there can be no pressure applied to the scent sacs. In other words, the animal needs a firm foothold to dispense its wares.

I have never tried the procedure.

Food habits? The skunk is omniverous and is generally considered beneficial in that it eats insects and rodents injurious to farmers. Part of the menu: Grasshoppers, crickets, cicadas, May beetles, wasps and larvae of different kinds. They love mice, wood rats, some ground nesting birds and eggs, lizards, turtles and turtle eggs, snakes, frogs, salamanders, fish, crustaceans and they will go for fruit. But they also will, on occasion, go for a farmer's chickens and, therefore, many toilers of the soil take a dim view of their existence.

While once their fur was considered useless, this is no longer the situation. This member of the weasel family, which may run five pounds or more, is trapped by the thousands, but Nature compensates by sponsoring litters of from four to seven youngsters, born in spring after a gestation period of about fifty days. The youngsters are well trained and a familiar sight is often seen — Mama leading her offspring, all in single file.

The animal sleeps during extreme cold but will leave the den in mild spells. The creature is a burrower and sometimes can be found occupying a home pad left vacant after the demise of its former woodchuck owner.

Unusual is the fact skunks can be tamed and become house pets, and enjoyable ones particularly after fear has been removed from humans — another way of saying scent sacs have been deactivated.

Nobody knows quite how or why Nature bestowed the described armament on the animal and about the only logical explanation is that once created, Nature must have looked at the creature and found that while it had claws and teeth, it was too amiable a waddler and needed additional protection.

Nature, probably feeling prankish, thereupon devised the sad sac system and told the animal to go forth and spray. Could be. Why not, pray tell? Have you a better explanation?

The skunk may well prove its might with many animals, but the great horned owl will choose it as prey, and the obnoxious odor obviously is ignored.

The Whistlepig

Characters of the field and woodlands, two woodchucks quite interested in the scene about them. Alert animals, they will vanish into their burrow if danger becomes reality. These are young 'chucks. In June or July the mother gives them the heave-ho with firm instructions they are on their own and had best seek new homes. Which, of course, they do.

The "American marmot" or woodchuck, also known as the groundhog or whistlepig, is a burrowing animal specializing in his own type of condominium, built where it most pleases, in field or forest, at low level or on a mountain slope.

You have, I am sure, seen the opening to a den — — a hole in the ground, about a foot wide, with excavated dirt piled in front. Possibly you have seen Old Flathead himself, half concealed in the entrance, gazing inquisitively at the world about, ready at a second's notice to take a dive for safety.

A diagram of the den complex proves the woodchuck is a cautious sort of fellow; the entrance makes a fairly abrupt drop of about a yard and then branches off into twenty to forty feet of branching galleries, with one or two ending in larger cavities lined with dried vegetation.

It is air-conditioned and the whistlepig pays not one cent to Niagara Mohawk Power Corp. or any other utility for current.

The conditioning comes in the fact that there are additional entrances (or exits), well concealed and without the tell-tale pile of dirt. These are known as "plunge holes," and for good reason. Literally they are escape hatches which the animal uses to preserve life and hide.

A woman gardener in Essex County about a year ago became understandably upset after watching her garden grow and disappear, with plants eaten off at the base. A friend placed a smoke bomb at the main entrance of the guilty party.

"That," he said confidently, "should do the trick." It didn't.

The chuck, sniffing the obnoxious vapor, merely departed by another exit and once the stench had cleared, resumed not only occupancy but feeding. The solution was not another bomb but a bullet. And the animal was buried, not hung upon a fence. Some believe a rotting carcass will keep other chucks distant. It will not, thus failing the intent of the shooter.

This member of the forest underground faces more enemies than Man. Its body is sought by predators such as the fox, coyote or bobcat. Man himself has not been kind. Farmers dislike him because of crop damage and he is often used as a living target by youngsters exercising their right to bear arms.

In New Hampshire, in 1883, a bounty of ten cents was placed on them, but there was an unusual stipulation: "Provided, That no bounty shall be paid for any woodchuck killed on Sunday!"

How proof was offered is yet to be determined. To the best of my knowledge, no woodchuck has yet signed his own death certificate, specifying date of death.

The animal's teeth also constitute danger of a most horrifying kind. The gnawing front teeth sometimes grow long and curve downward and upward, eventually and relentlessly piercing the skull and death is slow and painful.

Ordinarily considered a land-based animal, the chuck can also swim and climb trees. And it has astonishingly good eyesight; the eyes are set high on a somewhat flat head, and the rodent can detect movement several hundred yards distant.

It does possess certain benefits. For instance the den often is used not only by the original excavator but by skunks or cottontails. If chucks did not exist, the bunnies would diminish, since Big Ears is not a digger and, bereft of protection during the harsh chill of winter, cold could become the fatal scythe.

The whistlepig is a true hibernator, thus joining the chipmunk, bat and jumping mouse. When cold closes in, he (or she) descends into his home pad. And there the animal will pass into a deep sleep, with diminished body temperatures. If, for some reason, the winter chill penetrates the sanctuary and the temperature moves into the freezing point bracket, the chuck has a built-in warning mechanism. He awakens.

Hibernation continues for about six months or a little less and the little fat fella' who went to sleep will emerge with about one third of body weight lost. The loss is evident, since the chuck runs about ten pounds in normal weight.

Once out, it displays the tendency of a starved wolf. It will spend two to three weeks gorging on whatever green vegetation found to its liking. During this period the whistlepig pays less attention to predators and becomes easier prey.

If chucks are found wandering about during late snows, consider the reason as a romantical one. The wanderers are males in search of bed companions. Once mated, the sharing the den ceases; the female cares for the young in her own maternity ward and her lover, having done his duty, resumes a lonely existence in his own apartment.

The young number from three to nine, are born during April or May after a gestation period of just over 30 days. They will weigh about an ounce each, are blind and are born without a stitch of fur. Eyes open in about a month and fur develops in the meantime. The weaning process thereupon starts and in late June or early July the parent informs her sprouts they are on their own and had best start bringing in their own paychecks and digging their own tunnels.

Despite a clumsy appearance and an aura of stupidity, the woodchuck can, when cornered, become a fierce fighter; ask any fox with a bruised nose.

As vegetarians, their flesh, despite some opinions, makes good eating. Many game clubs, in preparing annual game stews, will include chunks of chuck. As a matter of fact, during the Great Depression, which began in October, 1929 and lasted until the 1930's, the whistlepig made up part of the menu for many unemployed who still retained use of a rifle.

And, of course, there is an interesting aspect to the name of whistlepig. The woodchuck's note is a short, shrill whistle when alarmed and often, during the same period, chatters its teeth.

That is fact. What isn't is the tale oft told, that the chuck places its "fingers" in its mouth to whistle!

A rarity; an albino woodchuck. While being white and fat may make a good picture, it bodes no rest for the animal. Reason: It is highly conspicuous and the easy-to-spot color draws predators.

An unusual photograph showing a woodchuck in actual hibernation. It was obtained by digging out the den; photo was taken quickly, since any change in temperature or environment will awaken a 'chuck from its deep sleep. Photo made by Walter J. Schoonmaker, an expert on the life of this strange and common animal.

The Comeback Kid

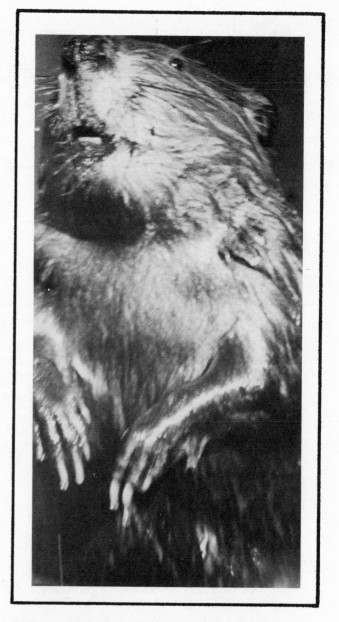

This sopping wet character, standing upright in the shallows of his pool, is figuring whether the photographer represents danger. The animal didn't think too long; seconds after the photo was snapped, the beaver took a dive to safety.

The brutal massacre, which began in the 1600's, was finally over in the late 1800's. The Adirondacks, once the home of hundreds of thousands of beaver, were literally stripped clean of this water-loving rodent almost one hundred percent.

What was believed to be inexhaustible proved otherwise. The beaver went the way of the western buffalo. Carcasses were shorn of hide and fur to satisfy the voracious appetite of vanity.

No animal could possibly withstand the relentless, inexorable pressure, the demands created by an overseas market supplied by Indian and white trappers who sold to the early Dutch.

In 1689 three beaver skins were worth one gun at the trading post, and the quality of that weapon was not of the best. For two skins, the Dutch paid trappers eight pounds of black powder or forty pounds of lead to be molded into musket balls.

Most appalling of all in this sad picture of extermination was that six hides were redeemable for six quarts of rum, and once imbibed, the Indian trapper paid a hangover price for weeks of hardship and toil, in all weather. Such was the "astuteness" of the early traders who piled up wealth on the degradation of the early native American.

Early Iroquoian castle (or village) sites excavated by archeologists up and down the Mohawk Valley disclosed tremendous numbers of broken rum bottles which once contained the alcoholic beverage. On one site, this writer saw thousands of pieces of bottles smashed after the contents had been drained dry.

And once bereft of the "rewards" of his toil, the Indian faced more lonely trips into the northern wilderness.

So for years and years the streams were undammed; beaver lodges rotted; dams were battered into oblivion by freshets and the sharp, explosive slap of beaver tails sounding warnings sounded no longer.

Bedeviled constantly, surviving beaver ceased making dams and lived in the banks of streams. A few were sighted in 1841 on the Indian and Cedar Rivers and at Tupper Lake. More sign was seen in the southern area of St. Lawrence County and the western portion of Essex County. Other survivors managed to stay alive only because they existed on private property, protected by owners.

The capture of one single beaver in 1880 on the Raquette River between Upper Saranac and Big Tupper Lake made news!

The overall picture was bleak; Man's avarice had done it again. Imperturable Nature cared not one damn.

Fortunately there were those who did care.

In 1903, eighteen years after the Forest Preserve became an actuality, the New York State Legislature, under pressure, came slightly to its senses. It appropriated the magnificent sum of $500 to begin the restoration of the beaver in the Adirondacks. The majesty of government, however, moved slowly to those days, even as it does today.

Typical scene in a beaver pool. The animal can be seen enjoying a swim, with the beaver lodge a backdrop. Sights such as the above are common but comparatively few individuals have enjoyed a look — managing one involves considerable patience, for the wild beaver is a wary individual, ready to take a dive at the slightest sign of danger.

It took two years for the purchase of three pairs from the American West. One pair was liberated in a small stream which entered the South Branch of the Moose River, and this twosome joined one surviving beaver which had migrated from the Woodruff Preserve, which had imported or managed to preserve a few from trappers and other enemies. The two additional pairs were given freedom in the northeast inlet of Big Moose Lake, but shortly thereafter migrated into the Beaver River area, some twenty miles distant. The reason is unknown. It could have been food supply.

In 1905, in a separate action, Edward Litchfield obtained and liberated a dozen beaver on his private preserve between Long Lake and Tupper Lake. As time went on some of these animals spread into new territory.

In the same year, the state Fish and Game Commission received a report of the existence of a "small, native colony of beavers, the last of the remnants of the original stock, inhabiting the waters northwest of Upper Saranac Lake."

The total number of the animals in the Adirondacks in 1905 was estimated as forty. That estimate came from the commission itself.

A small beginning of restoration, but a beginning.

The year 1906 saw the state legislature appropriating a healthier sum, $1,000, for more imports, and in 1907, seventeen were obtained from Yellowstone Park. The Adirondack census went up to one hundred in that year.

Better news developed as the years progressed. In 1914 the flat-tailed rodents were reported as multiplying rapidly "and taking possession of their ancient heritage in many different sections of the Adirondacks." Nature, working with Man, was cooperative.

The beaver is back today and in good numbers. In the 1930's, for instance, these non-graduates of engineering schools not only began to refill the North Country, but were moving into regions south, the Mohawk Valley for one, the same region emptied in early trapping days. One lodge was found in the old Erie Canal bed near the General Electric Company in the Town of Rotterdam. Another lodge was located in the Glenville hills by the late Percy Van Epps.

Earlier, in 1914, colonies were reported in the Colton area, Cranberry Lake, on the Oswegatchie River, at Still-water, West Canada Creek and scattered on streams in the Fulton Chain of lakes watershed. Seventy-nine colonies with 76 dams were noted in the latter area.

As a matter of fact, beaver were becoming nuisances at Eagle Creek. A state report stated that because of flooding a dam was torn down under direction of Game Protector Ball of Old Forge. The beaver rebuilt the barrier overnight.

"In another interesting case," the report stated, "the beaver insisted upon invading Dr. Nicholl's property on First Lake. Protector Ball placed a lighted lantern in a lodge of the intruders but they refused to take the hint to move on, and industriously extended their lodge over and around the warning beacon.

"Then in order to circumvent the trespassing beaver, the men put up a wire fence so the beaver could not get into Nicholl's yard where they were cutting poplars for food. Thereupon the wily animals vindicated the assertion of a scientist who said that 'beaver apparently depend more upon reason and less upon instinct than do the majority of the forest folk.'

"They piled wood against the fence and easily climbed over into the forbidden territory!"

The population moved into the Speculator area as well. Two dams were noted on the Miami River and colonies were observed on Whitney Creek. One large colony was observed on the North Branch of the Sacandaga River. Their presence was also noted at Newcomb, Raquette Lake, St. Regis and Long Lake.

Game Protector Butler of Long Lake reported that "the people living in this section think the beaver are doing fine and are glad to see them back. They tell me the beaver are a protection to our small streams containing trout, because the beaver builds dams and flood the marshes back of the dams. This makes it hard for the fishermen to fish all the pools and gives the trout a chance to grow."

Beaver numbered in the thousands about 1920. Resilience was thus proved.

One reason for the spread of population rested in the fact that when a colony became too large for the food supply, the younger element was ordered into new territory — and the order was enforced by older beaver, conscious of the fact that too many stomachs were on hand to digest bark.

The animal is comparatively large, with some adults reaching sixty pounds. They are considered the largest of North American rodents; are, of course, considered excellent engineers, building not only dams but lodges, the interiors reachable through underwater entrances. Natural enemies include the bobcat, wolf, fisher and, on occasion, the bear; there have been instances noted where bruin has tried his best to tear the lodge apart, but with no success, since the home is built of mud and interlacing sticks.

The animal mates in midwinter and a litter of from three to five are born in April or May with fur and with

The writer considers this a most unusual photo from the standpoint of time. It was taken in the 1930's and is of a beaver house in winter, only a few miles from the GE Company in Schenectady. Conservation Officer Chester Griffith is at right. Photo illustrates how quickly beaver spread after having been almost annihilated in the state.

open eyes. In about one month they leave the lodge to swim and eat of solid foods — leaves, twigs and bark. Among choices: Maple, willow, apple birch, poplar and alders. Clover and alfalfa are also consumed.

As a swimmer it is almost unmatchable; the hind feet are webbed and its lung capacity enormous. They store food, secreting it underwater in pool bottoms untouched by freezing. In many cases, as they enlarge feeding territories, they will build "canals" and transport meals in this fashion.

There remains one fallacy, however, which may need explaining.

Although they will topple sizeable trees and strip them clean of smaller branches, leaves and bark, they cannot anticipate the direction of fall. Thus unwary animals have, at times, been pinned under a crushing weight, helpless before any prowling predator. And there have been instances noted where trees gnawed at the base by teeth which never stop growing, have become hung against others.

In which case, Brother Flat Tail merely adopts a look of disgust, shrugs his shoulders, and starts gnawing on another.

There are no neurotics in this family.

Mr. Flattail himself, not an adult but one weighing about twenty pounds. Note richness of the fur, an excellent insulation against cold and wet.

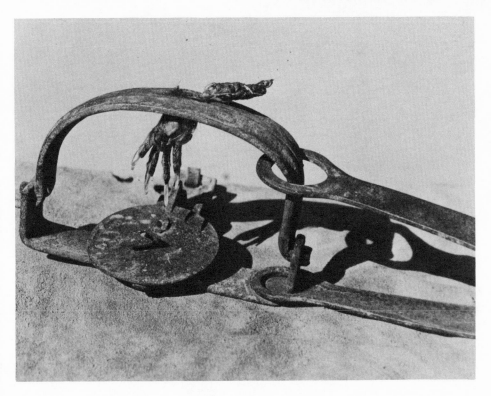

One of the tragedies which can befall a beaver; the remains of a foot in a trap. Two reasons could account for the scene. A predator could have devoured the helpless creature, or the beaver might have gnawed off its own foot. Trapping has been going on for centuries. It will not cease until there is no demand for the hides.

THE "POND DOG" (BEAVER)

A drawing rather difficult to explain. It refers to the "Pond Dog," or American beaver, and was sketched by an "artist" who probably relied upon verbal description rather than reality. Drawing is taken from an old print, dated 1755. Note the pond dog's housing complex with entrance at ground level and a second story window through which to observe life abounding around!

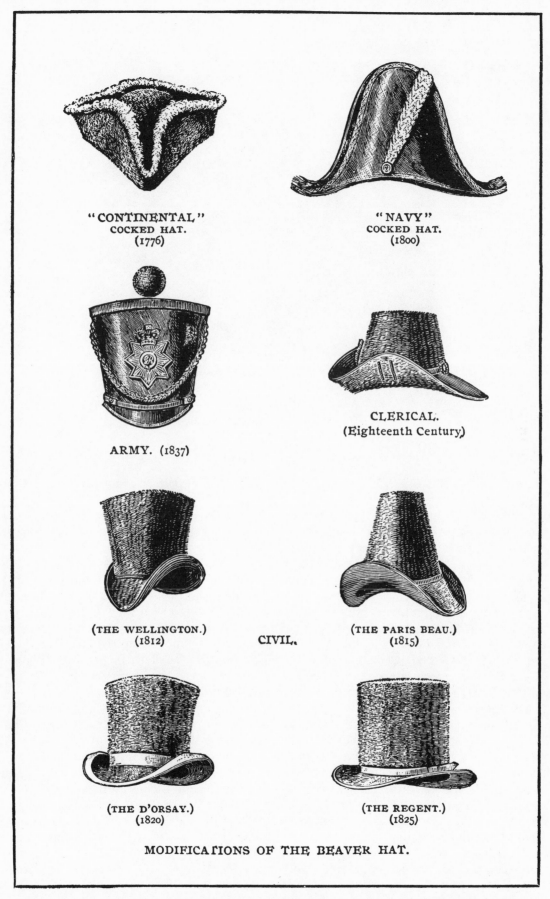

"CONTINENTAL"
COCKED HAT.
(1776)

"NAVY"
COCKED HAT.
(1800)

ARMY. (1837)

CLERICAL.
(Eighteenth Century)

(THE WELLINGTON.)
(1812)

CIVIL.

(THE PARIS BEAU.)
(1815)

(THE D'ORSAY.)
(1820)

(THE REGENT.)
(1825)

MODIFICATIONS OF THE BEAVER HAT.

While the above illustrates types of beaver hats made from the soft fur and pressed into felt the animal had other uses. Skins were used in manufacture of glue and the castoreum, a secretion found in two sacs in the genital area was valued as a medicine. In the late 1790's castoreum came into use as bait for beaver and was used in steel traps, which came into existence about that time.

The Coyote

The Eastern coyote, of the type now roaming the Adirondacks, and considered by many as a deer predator.

The early Aztecs called them coyotl.

The early Spanish who invaded Central America and the early American West corrupted the name to coyote. And that is what the animal is best known as today.

Another designation, seldom used, is the prairie wolf.

No one knows exactly how this species arrived in New York State, but most assuredly the coyote is here and here to stay. It has, in its native canniness, mastered the ability to remain close to Man despite hunting pressures. And other than Man there are few natural enemies. Disease can be counted among them.

As far as dogs are concerned, there are very few adroit enough to run down a coyote and in battle the animal is equal to any dog of comparable size.

How long has this immigrant been in New York State? Once again, an open question. But in the early 1930's, when this writer discussed the subject with the late John Halpin, Conservation Department Commissioner, I was told the animal was being reported with increasing frequency by game protectors. Other individuals reported the coyote as a wolf, a not unusual mistake, since the coyote in appearance resembles a small wolf or a German shepherd dog.

In comparison with the timber wolf, the coyote skull is smaller and lighter. The canine teeth are, oddly enough, relatively longer and slighter. In the manner of walking, the wolf will hold its bushy tail more upright than the coyote. In size there is no comparison; the wolf is much larger.

There are several versions as to how the coyote became a resident of this state. One of the most common is that pups were brought in by travelers, held as pets, then either escaped or were released. The animal can be tamed.

Another version is that the coyote migrated from Canada, specifically Ontario and those in that province migrated from the western areas of southern Canada and northern United States during the 1920's, following railroad rights-of-way and highway routes. Poisoning was a popular pasttime during the late 1800's and during the 20th century. The horrific practice still remains in many areas of the West where the mammal is considered a menace to livestock.

In Canada their presence was first noted in the great number of pelts traded at Hudson Bay Company stores throughout northern and central Ontario.

In discussing range movement, it is logical to assume that once settled in that province, it was a simple matter to migrate from the northern shores of the St. Lawrence River into the northern Adirondacks, with the crossing of the water barrier done on its frozen surface.

On the matter of mating: This takes place during late winter and the gestation period for pups is about sixty days. A litter consists usually of from five to ten youngsters, all born blind and quite helpless. They are well cared for by both parents and the family breaks up during the fall. From then on the new generation is on its own.

A coyote, perfectly willing to eat what it finds, sniffs out food in a picnic area where previous tenants have managed to do what too many do — leave wrappers, cans and other trash scattered about.

The coyote has been known to mate with dogs and the result is the "coy-dog." Some of the hybrids resulting are large in size and lead many to believe that the dog-coyote mixture may eventually lead into a wild species replacing the true wolf. Whatever the ultimate outcome, the coyote has an interesting history.

Animals of similar size and shape once roamed the North American continent during the period when the sabre-tooth tiger and mastodon existed. Some feel the coyote resembles the jackals of the Eastern Hemisphere (Europe, Africa, Asia and Australia). There are others who feel there is a relationship. Could be.

In New York State the coyote range is expanding. They are no longer residents of the forest alone. They have moved into farmlands; their sharp yapping or wailing can be heard in such counties as Saratoga or Fulton. They have learned to be wary of Man but to live side-by-side.

In seeking food the coyote usually is a loner. It is rare to find a group and if one is sighted harassing a white-tail marooned it usually is a family group. There is no need for group cooperation generally, since the coyote, unlike the wolf, subsists mainly on small game. The usual fare would include mice, squirrels, woodchucks, rabbits and hares.

Carrion is not overlooked. Birds are included on the menu when the animal is quick enough to grab one. Snakes are eaten. As a matter of fact, one enemy of the rattlesnake on the Tongue Mt. range at Lake George is the coyote. To kill a rattler is an evidence of the speed and skill of the predator.

The prairie wolf is a denner, digging its own, or expanding dens created by other in-ground dwellers. Dens may be found not only in forested areas, well concealed, but as mentioned, on farm properties.

Adult males may run as high as fifty-five pounds or slightly more, but this is considered unusual. The weight range of from twenty-five to fifty pounds is more common. The average dead coyote seen by this writer has usually weighed in at about thirty-five pounds.

TIMBER WOLF

FOR COMPARISON

COYOTE

98

Mr. Monkey Mitts

Raccoons, awake or asleep, active or inactive, always make for fine photographs. These two curious animals prove the point by giving their all for the camera.

Tired after a day of canoeing, I bedded down for the night on a promontory in Northwest Bay, Lake George, and left a small cache of cleaned and scaled sunnies in a basin of lake water on a small bench, ready to fry up for breakfast.

Foolish Man.

About 2 a.m. I was awakened by a chattering and the crash of the basin onto rock. Directing a flashlight beam on the scene I was not too surprised to find two raccoons raiding the cache. Grabbing the nearest object, which happened to be a moccasin, I yelled and flung that article at the animals. They lumbered away.

Back to sleep. Hours later more noise and the reappearance of the persistent pair. I yelled once again, tossed the other moccasin. The twosome pulled another vanishing act.

By this time light was showing and I struggled out of my sleeping bag. Half the fish were gone. In stocking feet I searched for my moccasins and thereupon learned an unpleasant fact.

In placing the sleeping bag, my feet were pointed toward the lake. The bench was thus between my feet and the water. Both moccasins had sailed over the raccoons, over the rocky shoreline and landed in twenty feet of water! Not only landed, but disappeared. After turning the air a gentle blue, I put on an extra pair of moccasins I had brought along and performed breakfast chores. As far as I'm concerned, the original pair still rests on submerged state property.

Anyone who has camped in the woods or owns a cottage along a stream or lakefront can spill raccoon stories by the dozen. As a source of stories this animal knows few equals.

The raccoon is mostly nocturnal and does a lot of traveling for food — and food means almost everything. Fish are a delight. So are crayfish, fresh water clams, frogs, lizards, turtles, birds and eggs, nuts, fruits, raw meat and almost anything which grows in a farmer's fields. Corn is particularly sought and the warfare between farmer and raccoon is ceaseless.

Trying to keep this mammal out of a cornfield is a frustrating job. One example: Devices which create blasts at regular intervals have been set in cornfields to frighten the animal. The noise means nothing after a time. The raccoon gets accustomed to it and since he sees no predator nor does he scent one, he continues his pilferage.

Farmers may consider them pests but many individuals consider them pets. They can be tamed up to a point. The writer has raised young raccoons from an early age, found them fascinating. But I have had the help of a female dog who, with commendable maternal instinct literally adopted them.

I cannot prove that raccoons will answer to command, since my own procedure in photographing ones made into pets has been to include the dog. In the woodlands the dog answered to command. The raccoon (or raccoons) did what the dog did. Thus a whistle brought on the entire entourage. This procedure worked extremely well both on land and in the water, since the animals are powerful swimmers and followed the dog with ease, often at times swimming alongside.

I did, however, keep some degree of peace by feeding them from separate plates. They played well together, in mock ferociousness, but I took no chances when food was involved.

Raccoons will grow to weigh as much as twenty to twenty-five pounds and they handle their bulk skillfully. In water they are considered the master of any dog and quite able to drown one. Their teeth are nothing to ignore and they inflict a nasty bite.

This I know. I did a stint on WRGB-TV some years ago with one of my pets and for some reason it considered my arm an ear of corn, starting gnawing. Playful, perhaps, but not to the victim, who had to maintain a steady contenance before the camera while trying to separate the animal from an arm.

It is impossible not to be able to identify this woodland beast. The fur, or pelage, is heavy and thick; it wears a facial mask of black; its front and hind feet have five toes each and the tail is bushy and ringed.

To watch a raccoon feed is a lesson in expertise. The five toes on each of the front feet are long and slender and can be manipulated with the finesse of human digits. The animal can lift the top off a garbage can to get at delectables within. It can undo simple knots. It is baffled by a padlock, but perhaps Nature will take care of that lack eventually.

Whether it "washes" its food is open to argument. I have fed my own pets on dry land and no effort was made to seek water. If anything, I feel the "washing" procedure is based upon observation of a raccoon seeking crayfish or clams; the method is for the animal to stand in shallow water and search the bottom with its forepaws. When it hits pay dirt, it grabs.

Home is in the trees, in dens, or in large fissures in rock. The animal is an expert climber and can master any size tree. Such growth is not the only sanctuary sought, however. There have been instances of cottage owners firing up fireplaces and becoming blinded by smoke, the cause of which was a raccoon in the chimney!

The mammal mates in late January or early February and in about sixty days Mama brings forth three to six young, covered with fur; the eyes do not open until three weeks have passed. The young are taught the wisdom of the wild until fall, and are capable of mating within a year of birth.

Mr. Monkey Mitts, or The Masked Robber — names applied — evidences strong intelligence and cunning and proof of possession of these qualities rest in the fact that the animal remains in goodly numbers despite hunting pressures and natural enemies.

Thus he is another animal which has managed to live almost side-by-side with Man even, at times, within the confines of a city. Credit him for that, even if he eats your corn!

Mr. Mushsquash

A muskrat home, a familiar sight to many who travel swamplands. Much labor goes into the making; that is an obvious fact, and in its interior the 'rat, or mushsquash as it was known in early days, lives a comfortable life.

Find a pond or marsh and you'll probably discover that among its occupants is an animal which once was served in restaurants as the "marsh rabbit."

One slight difficulty, however. It resembles the rabbit in shape and temperament about as much as an armadillo resembles a moose.

The "marsh rabbit" is, in reality, the muskrat or "mushsquash," a fur-bearing, plant eater about three to four times the size of the common rat. The nearest kin seems to be the short-tailed field mice, also found in abundance in wet meadows.

Find the muskrat and you'll also find that this water-loving animal has no financial worries when it comes to building a home or condominium. High interest rates bother him not one whit. Mortgages are of no import. When the buck rat wants a home he flexes his muscles, trots out his do-it-thyself kit and builds one. No contractors — not even the beaver — are involved.

Once a big mound is constructed of cattails and other vegetation, plus a bit of mud skillfully applied here and there, he hollows it out, using excavated materials to do more plastering outside. Once completed, the 'rat may bring in selected friends and colleagues; as many as ten may live within the dome.

This unusual animal, peculiar to North America — but spread by Man in Europe — is numbered in the untold millions.

It is heavily trapped for fur but reproduces at such a rate that numbers never seem to diminish. A swamp may literally be cleared and within a short time once again will be occupied. Even man-made ponds are spotted by the alert 'rat and utilized. One might add that lodges are built not in deep areas, but shallow ones. No dam is constructed.

The first litter is born in late April or early May and production continues right on through the season, until several litters have replenished the population. The gestation period is usually about one month. It takes little more than that length of time for the young to start doing their own thing in the world. Litters may number up to thirteen.

The population of this water dweller needs this constant replenishment. Man does not live by fear alone, to corrupt a common saying. But the muskrat apparently does. He is a tid-bit to many predators. From the blueness of a tranquil sky sweeps the marsh hawk. From the blackness above, at night, glides the great horned owl with its deadly talons.

The voracious mink is a constant threat to peace of mind because of this animal's ability to enter the domed house and create its usual scene of carnage and woe. Large turtles, such as snappers, will feast upon the creature. So do water snakes. Bobcats make their kills. The coyotes do the same. Raccoons aren't too far behind and the larger northern pike, if in the vicinity, will swim over and do an equally deadly job on the smaller 'rats.

Not a pleasant life but, one imagines, an interesting one.

Animals kill the muskrat for food. Once Man did. But that seems to be a thing of the past. Today Man kills for fur and the muskrat is considered only as a valuable fur animal. It is interesting to note that more than ten million skins were sold in London as far back as 1914 and millions more were sold in America during the same year. Vast numbers of skins were shipped out of Albany ports during the 1700's to foreign countries. Equally interesting is that in 1905 the muskrat was introduced by Man to Europe — and promptly spread.

They are not mountain climbers; high peaks are free from them. But they do live in the lowlands, wherever there is suitable water environment. In earlier days furriers, annoyed with describing them as muskrats, started referring to the pelts as Hudson seal, river mink or ondatra mink, whatever that meant. In earlier days the flesh was considered a tasty dish, and once again, disguise came into the picture; the name "marsh rabbit" was applied.

(In a way, this should not be considered too unusual in the field of gastronomy. The common English sparrow at one time was called the "reed bird" and these tiny importees were sold by the pound. The sparrow fell into disfavor, however, when its habit of following the horses became well known).

By habit nocturnal, the muskrat will vary its lifestyle by moving about during the day. Food consists of roots and stems, fresh water clams, sometimes a fish or two and, if near farmlands, they will swim ashore and partake of delicacies thereon. The cattail plant is high on their list of favorite foods.

Any water animal faces a decided threat in winter. When a sheath of ice covers pond or marsh, the mushsquash creates an air, or breather hole and to keep it open will often plug it with waste food material. Access to the outer world is thus maintained.

All in all, a remarkable animal, stupid to be sure, but smart enough to exist alongside of Man. The odds have long been against the 'rat's survival but so far he has beaten them.

Production Expert

"They breed like rabbits."

A timeworn phrase and a popular one based on fact. And the bunny called the cottontail rabbit is the subject of such comment.

The cottontail hardly can be considered the best example of planned parenthood in the thickets, swamps and hedgerows in which it abounds.

The assembly line run by Nature in the manufacture of these small and frisky mammals is a never ceasing one. The cottontail is a creature built on a foundation of misfortune. Although possessing four "lucky rabbit feet" the animal is killed by the millions annually in the United States, not only by natural predators, but Man and, in a way, Man might fit into that descriptive category. Replacement models, however, new to the world but not new in size, color or shape, keep flowing to maintain the population.

If anything keeps the population from overruning the country, it would be disease.

No cottontail mother that I know of has ever gone on strike, taken to the pill or subscribed to the population zero philosophy. Several litters, usually containing three to six young, are produced over the breeding season of spring and summer. Mama seems to spend more time in the woodsy boudoir than in the kitchen.

The young are born after a gestation period of about thirty days, blind, almost naked, each weighing less than an ounce. They mature rapidly to make way for the next batch, never slow in coming. Born usually in a small, natural cavity in the earth, they rest on a lining of grasses and soft fur which the mother plucks from her underside. The nests are covered with grass or leaves and almost impossible to detect.

Mama, ever the considerate soul, returns at dusk and dawn, opens the enclosure and nurses the young — provided, of course, she doesn't meet up with a predator looking for a quick lunch.

The nest itself is a masterpiece of camouflage; may exist under shrubbery, on lawns, in thickets and brushpiles. But even with the camouflage, the young are subject to the usual terrors of Nature — embodied in the fact that they furnish food for such animals and birds as the fox, skunk, coyote, bobcat, opossum, the owl and

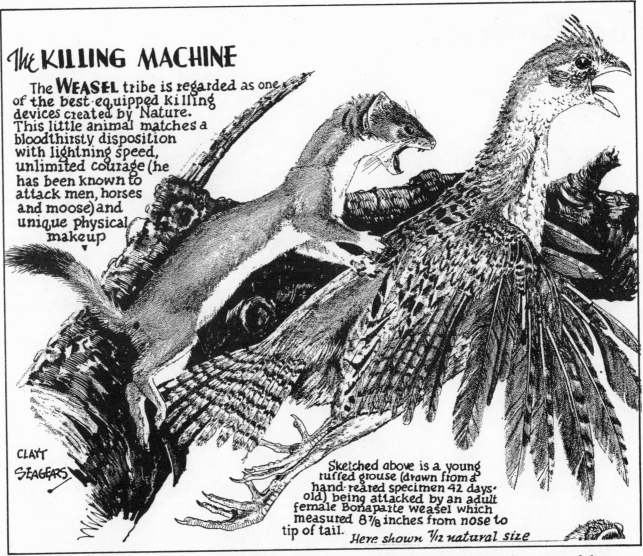

THE KILLING MACHINE

The **WEASEL** tribe is regarded as one of the best-equipped killing devices created by Nature. This little animal matches a bloodthirsty disposition with lightning speed, unlimited courage (he has been known to attack men, horses and moose) and unique physical makeup ▼

CLAYT SEAGEARS

Sketched above is a young ruffed grouse (drawn from a hand-reared specimen 42 days old) being attacked by an adult female Bonaparte weasel which measured 8⅞ inches from nose to tip of tail. *Here shown ½ natural size*

Self explanatory is this fine sketch by Clayt Seagears, and which is reproduced through courtesy of the Conservationist Magazine. The weasel is pictured attacking a ruffed grouse. But the weasel also will seek out and kill cottontails. Seagears rightly calls this animal a "killing machine". It is. Sometimes it kills for the sake of killing.

the hawk. The young have been known to be devoured by the larger snakes. Nothing nice about this, but that is The Order of Things in the environment surrounding them.

Oddly enough, the rabbit is not without voice. The small ones can utter cries of alarm, tiny squeaks of terror. The older rabbits, faced with the inevitable when a weasel tightens its death grip, literally will shriek. It is not a pleasant sound; it is as though the mute are calling out in agony for help which never arrives.

The cottontail range is spreading. At one time it was a stranger in northern New York State. But it is moving into the southern regions and sightings farther north are not unusual. It is not a deep woods animal, but it will move into areas which have been lumbered. And it does not thrive in open fields; it is too wary, too timid. It is not considered a "digger," but during winter months it will seek out and occupy abandoned burrows of the woodchuck or some other animal gifted with the ability to excavate its own home.

Build a garden if you wish to encourage occupancy in your neighborhood. The cottontails adore young plants such as peas, radishes, lettuce and beans and can clean out rows in a jiffy. Ask any apoplectic gardener who has discovered such devastation. In the winter, sumac bark is a delicacy, as well as buds and twigs of small shrubbery or tree growth. Wrapping a newly planted tree, for instance, is a wise move.

There are some who consider the cottontail one of the most important small game animals in the state. Such a conclusion is logical, since the flesh is tender and tasty.

In any discussion of the bunny it would be remiss to ignore one rather peculiar eating habit. If you spot a cottontail busy in clover or any other green food, consider the fact that what is eaten is swallowed. And later the rabbit will seek a sanctuary where it can defecate greenish pellets. This is not waste matter, but food which has not been digested. They are eaten.

The Redcoat

Lifelike to an amazing degree is this mounting of a red fox, paw uplifted, eyes intent upon possible food. Wide in range, the red fox evidences unusual intelligence for an animal; often outwits pursuers such as dogs.

The author, driving in the southern Adirondacks one bright day, slowed his car, then stopped to observe a sight seldom seen.

In a nearby field a red fox had made a successful leap upon a rabbit and, once enclosed in its strong jaws, there was a shaking of the victim, then a trotting off into a patch of woods nearby, there to ingest and digest.

The fox is here to stay, Man or no Man, hunting or no hunting. It is an animal noted for its cunning, a resident of settled areas and one of the forest as well as fields. I have seen them walking trails in the Miami River area, between Speculator and Indian Lake, a heavily wooded tract. And I have seen them walking slowly along a stone fence in farm country, not more than one hundred yards from the owner's home.

They require no special menu. They prey upon woodchucks, common rats, field mice, poultry, carrion, birds, eggs, snakes, turtles, grasses, berries, wild cherries, musk-rats, grapes, insects, young raccoons and, at times, even a young and comparatively helpless fawn.

The animal is easily recognizable; is about the size of a small dog and the average adult weight ranges from ten to eleven pounds. Heavier weights are considered unusual.

The nose is pointed, the ears prominent, the tail long and bushy. The fur is rich; they are shy but have been tamed.

Mating occurs in the spring and about fifty days later a litter of up to nine or ten are born. The pups remain in the den — sometimes in a woodchuck den "abandoned" by the 'chuck through sudden death applied by the aspiring occupant — for a few weeks, then appear to frolic and learn the facts of life topside. Both parents feed and care for the offspring.

The family splits in late summer and the young, by this time trained in the ways of the wild, move to other territorial domains. The parents apparently pair for life and the only divorce is death.

Cute fox pups sun themselves at the entrance to their den, a burrow in an open field. These two are probably resting from a long period of play as well as a battle over scraps of meat and bones delivered to them by a fond mother.

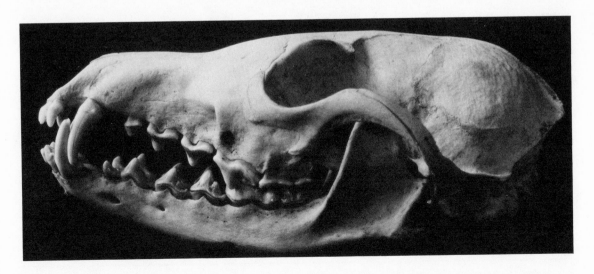

Skull of a red fox, with an excellent view of its major weapons — teeth. Jaw muscles can exert remarkable power and the fox is lightning fast.

An interesting sketch by the late Walter Schoonmaker showing a red fox looking over the situation before making a leap upon an unsuspecting mouse. Mice form a good share of the diet of a fox — which also includes woodchucks, birds, eggs, snakes and even, at times a slow-moving turtle.

Fleetfoot

Two whitetails make an attractive picture as they move slowly through winter snows in the Adirondacks. Photo taken during early winter, evidenced by condition of the animals. As the season's harshness descends, deer suffer greatly from lack of food sources and predation. It is not a pleasant phase of their existence.

Here are some commonly asked questions about the white-tailed deer:

Q: When do fawns lose their white spots?
A: Usually in late summer.

Q: Is the white-tail a browser or grazer?
A: It is considered a browser but on some occasions will condescend to graze.

Q: Is the animal nocturnal only?
A: Not so. It is active at all hours although there is less movement during daytime.

Q: How often do bucks (males) grow antlers?
A: Annually. It is a marvel of Nature. Full size is usually attained in about four months. After carrying the antlers for several months, and using them in battles for a harem, the antlers drop naturally; are shed from late December to February; there is no set, rigid time.

During early growth they are in "velvet," that is a "true skin," which is rubbed off by the animal.

Q: Are antlers an indication of age?
A: No. Age of a white-tail is usually determined by teeth and wear.

Q: Are twins or triplets unusual?
A: Not in the case of an adult doe.

Q: Can the white-tail swim?
A: It is an expert one.

Q: Why is the animal known as the white-tail?
A: The question is easily answered if one sees a deer in flight. The tail is held upright showing a white fur underside.

* * * * * *

By and far the creature under discussion is the most valuable of the big game which roams the Adirondack forest. It exists as such along with the black bear but far less of the latter is present.

At one time the white-tails were almost exterminated in the entire Northeast; from the earliest of days they were hunted relentlessly not only for food but for the hides. In Colonial days one skin could be traded for one loaf of bread. The hide, furthermore, can be tanned into

what is known as buckskin, and clothing made from such was commonly worn.

Even today in modern shops, buckskin can be split into thin layers and made into shirts, dresses, bikinis and even formal evening gowns! It is soft and water does not destroy shape. An early belief that fringes on jackets would help drain off rain water led to those decorations but the added efficiency is open to question.

Merciless hunting and winter kill in 1870-1880 almost killed off the deer not only in the Adirondacks but in

In 1896 this raw "sport" was outlawed. Scene is portrayed in a sketch hanging in the New York State Museum, Albany; represents a common practice in days of yore when dogs hounded deer on snow and men, on snowshoes, made the kill. What happened when the dogs finally cornered the white-tail before the hunters arrived leaves much to the imagination.

the entire state. In 1886 the first bag limit was established; three deer per person. Before this time any number could be slaughtered for personal or market use. In 1895 the season was established from August 11 to October 31, and the bag limit reduced to two animals per person. In 1912 the buck-only law was passed, which meant only antlered white-tails could be killed.

The year 1886 saw the law prohibiting taking (shooting) deer over crusted snow — the animals have great difficulty in negotiating this type of snow cover and in flight often lacerate their legs. The year 1896 saw hounding by dogs prohibited and the year after that a law was passed prohibiting jacking, or hunting deer by artificial light. Thus the progress over the years, and the deer have responded by increasing their numbers tremendously.

Bucks have been known to run as high as three-hundred pounds or slightly more, but such weights are unusual. Hunting pressures keep age levels down. So do

pressures exerted by predators such as bobcats, which prey upon smaller or weakened deer, coyotes and, of course, the domestic dog running wild in packs during winter months when the white-tails are comparatively helpless because of deep or crust snows.

Automobiles have become major killers; thousands are killed on state highways annually; deer crossing signs seem to be of little avail in protection, even though they mark ancient trails in existence long before highways came into being.

Winter starvation, or winter kill is another major killer. Deer "yard up" in the cold months, consume all food reachable within their small domain. As food diminishes, so does weight. So does strength. The animals easily become exhausted.

The legal deer kill in New York State over a decade can be estimated in the hundreds of thousands. There is no estimate of illegal killing but this is a major factor also.

Mating occurs in and around November, when the air chills and the nights turn crisp, and the young are dropped in late May or June. Gestation period is about seven months. The rutting (mating) season is a violent one for bucks because this is the period when savage battles occur for the favor of does. Battles are sometimes fought to the death in that antlers lock and the hyped-up animals become helpless; the struggle then becomes one for survival, not mates, and if there is no separation, the fighters die a slow death of starvation or from attacks of predators, ever on the alert for the weakened.

This beautiful animal is an accurate marksman with hoofs, successful at times in decapitating a rattler. A blow from a hoof can lead to injury; ask any conservation officer who has felt the impact. One officer known to the author attempted to rescue what he considered a worn-out doe from a lake into which she had been chased by dogs. In attempting to lift her, one hoof flashed and his breeches were cut from waist to knee, leaving a raw wound on his leg. In later attempts, with other deer, he learned to hog-tie the creature.

Food? The white-tail will eat herbs on dry land and lily pads and other pond or lake plants in water. Acorns, beechnuts and other mast are consumed; during winter the animal will browse upon buds and twigs of maples, white cedar, some conifers and birch. Often in yards trees will be trimmed evenly at a certain height. This is the level the tallest of the deer can reach while rearing on its hind legs. In some instances the trees appear as though they had been trimmed neatly by power hedge trimmers.

As this chapter is written, New York State has an over abundance and as a result, a so-called "doe season" has become legal. At the same time, in sections other than the Adirondacks or Catskills, the season is being opened because of heavy damage caused by deer to orchards. Hungry deer can ruin a year's new growth on an apple tree in short order. And they can damage other crops with equal ability.

One story remains outstanding in the author's memory. It is worth the retelling.

During World War Two research was being done on female deer at what was then known as the Delmar Game Farm, maintained in the Albany area by the Conservation Department. Male hormones were placed in small incisions made in animals' bodies and the incisions were then closed. The females began to grow "antlers" or unusual bone growth, and not always on heads. One did reportedly grow a good sized rack in proper position.

The times were such that meat was rationed in food markets. One night poachers invaded the pen at Delmar, killed the antlered doe and made off with her carcass.

Promptly a news release was issued, one of warning. It explained that the effect of the male hormone injected was NOT known upon humans, and the meat

A deer yard, the domain of the white-tails during the harshness of winter. During this period the animals are highly susceptible to starvation and attacks by predators – including the domestic dog, which wears another hat, that as a member of a roving pack. Dogs attacking deer during this period (and others) can be shot on sight by lawmen. As a matter of fact many have been shot by non-lawmen.

should NOT be eaten. And it warned that if the poacher or poachers involved consumed any of the meat, and bone growth began on their heads, they had best seek medical attention!

Good story, but nobody reported a growth of antlers and the case was never solved.

Another method of obtaining a kill in the days when almost any kind of hunting was contenanced. This sketch, seen by visitors at the New York State Museum, represents a regular activity of some hunting parties – driving a deer into the water and then using it as a target while it swims desperately to save its life. There were also "hunters" who overtook a swimming white-tail and literally clubbed it into unconsciousness.

A sight of grace and speed. Alerted to danger the deer takes off in a giant leap, its tail held upright, thus showing the "white flag" typical of the animal in the Adirondacks and other areas of the state.

A winter's scene oft enacted in areas where white-tails roam. In this photo, taken by Capital Newspapers Photographer Skip Dickstein, a deer has been chased by dogs onto the ice of Hudson's River. Two dogs, one at upper right corner, rest, eyeing the exhausted animal. It is believed, however, the two dogs pictured were not the outlaws doing the chasing; they happened upon the scene after others had driven the deer on ice and then vanished. That was the reason the above dogs were not shot by a conservation officer.

A starry-eyed fawn, only a few weeks old, stands on somewhat spindly legs, but ones which will grow into powerful appendages to carry the animal to safety or to use as deadly weapons.

114

Death comes in many forms in the forest. And death leaves in physical form what once was alive and a thing of beauty. It is not unusual to find carcasses of the white-tails, victims of winter kill, starvation or the hunter's gun. In the latter instance, the deer is not felled immediately but runs from the hunter, to collapse at a later time. It is to the credit of most hunters that they will spend a great deal of time trying to locate a wounded animal.

115

An Animal Most Grotesque

Quotes, past and present, on the moose:
From zoologist J.E. DeKay in the mid 1800's:

"They are yet numerous in the unsettled portions of the state, in the counties of Essex, Hamilton, Herkimer, Franklin, Lewis and Warren, and since the gradual removal of the Indians they are now (1841) believed to be on the increase."

Frederick J.H. Merriam, director of the New York State Museum in 1899, spoke in a different theme:

"It is not many years since the moose (Alce americanus) was a favorite object of pursuit in the Adirondacks, from which region it was exterminated as nearly as I can ascertain in about the year 1861."

Now for a quote, more modern; this one made in November, 1981, by Commissioner Robert F. Flacke, Department of Environmental Conservation:

"Moose are still present in northern New York. It is believed these are the same animals that migrated across Lake Champlain from Vermont in 1980. These rare movements began in June and continued through early October.

"Last year several dozen big game hunters observed moose tracks while others caught glimpses of the animals eating, walking and running through dense forest cover. Fortunately none were mistaken for deer and all survived the northern New York hunting seasons."

The moose sighted, all separately, consisted of three cows and two bulls. They were reported in the following areas:

Clinton County near Redford; Franklin County between St. Regis Falls and Loon Lake; Hamilton County between Indian Lake and Speculator; Herkimer County near Old Forge and St. Lawrence County near Sevey's Corners. No calves were seen.

In the early 1950's this writer heard of a sighting along Route 3, north of Coreys, which is southwest of Saranac Lake. I drove to the area to photograph tracks in the highway shoulder. The individual who witnessed the bull saw it descend from an embankment, cross the road and start trotting eastward. The witness, driving, slowed, then pushed the accelerator and along with the car the moose increased it speed, traveling several hundred yards along the shoulder until it decided it had enough of the highway, and vanished into the woods.

So the question remains: Do the moose more recently sighted plan to remain or are they to be considered wanderers?

A few years ago a moose named Amos by the Willsboro Fish and Game Club, died near Willsboro, Essex County. He had been sighted, obviously, earlier and was presumed to be a wanderer from Canada and his trail had him passing through Vermont. Reportedly a man named Harold Barber came upon him swimming just off the Vermont shore across from Ticonderoga.

Amos was a young bull. He was later punctured by a bullet expelled from a rifle held by a hunter who mistook him for a deer. The death scene was about seventy miles south of the Canadian border.

A sad story, but that's the way the bullet bounces on occasion.

The animal is totally protected in New York State; anyone convicted of killing one is subject to a maximum fine of $2,000, a year in jail or both. The law was signed March 29, 1980, by Gov. Hugh Carey following an incident which occurred in the Broadalbin area of Fulton County where a youth reportedly shot a wandering bull, minding its own business in a field. While the moose was protected even then there seemed to be confusion over penalty; the amendment to the new law rectified the situation.

As noted elsewhere, it is entirely possible that this big, grotesque member of the deer family may well return permanently to former Adirondack haunts, particularly in the wilderness areas where motorized traffic is forbidden and thus where the hunter must use his or her feet. The moose is considered a deep woods animal, frequenting growths of spruce, tamarack, birch, aspen and alders. These enormous beasts, weighing well over a half ton at full growth, have no fear of water, are often seen where they exist in number, standing in shallows, sometimes up to their necks, feeding on water plants. They will submerge completely to obtain the food and a five to six-foot spread of palmated antlers, mounted on an enormous head, rising from the depths, cascading water, is a spectacular sight.

So is a charging moose. During the mating season in late fall, when the males are full of defiance, they have been known to attempt to run down hunters.

The last family of moose was destroyed by gunshot in 1861 in the Raquette Lake region. The last known single survivor was killed along the Marion River by a guide named Palmer. It was a cow.

Apparently the beast is not noted for its intelligence nor does it possess an ability to select "bed mates." Several years ago a wanderer, presumably from the north, was sighted in the Troy area, then in Columbia County. Its presence on the land of a dairy farmer became well known when it attempted to leap a six-foot fence to join some heifers. I understand the farmer promptly placed his stock in a barn. The bull supposedly suffered from a condition known as "brain worms," but diseased or not, it managed to leap the fence!

This big animal with the big nose is considered the large cousin of the elk of the northern forests of Europe and Siberia.

Hopefully the "wanderers" sighted recently in the Adirondacks — if wanderers they be — will remain for keeps. And remain, of course, under full protection.

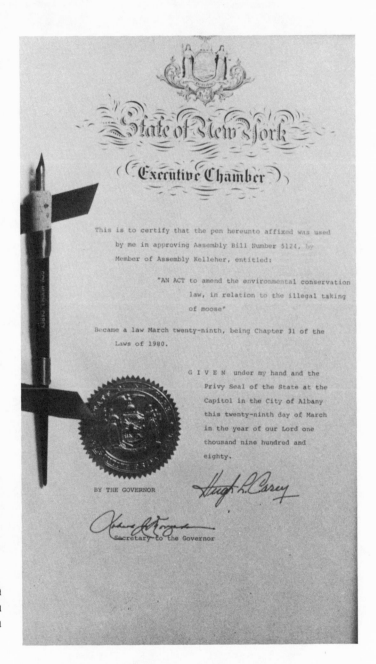

The pen used in signing the amendment to the conservation law specifying total protection (and penalties) for the killing of a moose in New York State. Pen and certificate presented to Assemblyman Neil Kelleher, Troy, who introduced the bill.

What once was offered travelers in the Adirondacks: Cow moose and offspring, above, and a bull moose spending leisure time half submerged in a pond. Scenes were not photographed in the North Country, but illustrate times as once they were.

A Hanging Matter

Done--History of the Crime and its Progress in the Courts.

to find any
ce of death
on her. The
he legislature
of the unfor-
but without
eel that her
lack of effort
Everything
them though
ecution this
and most un-

ge 'number
that her life
it those peo-
by sentiment
a sad and sol-
of a human
the law, but
is the crime,
Law is found
teat
is a sacred
the law's ex-
this case the
ed and wan-

er home may
y have suff-
ty, justified

associations,
besides repre-
papers pres n

Saturday
George Was
from his ho
last farewell
emotion wh
did Georgie
wore off, an
concernedly
day occurrer
ly to be exc
illustrates th
he was brou
a boy who c
checkers ne
very instant
being burne
ence in bit
soon to expi

was a restle
did not fall
and then
o'clock she
dressed hers
to eat until
morning, w
oyster soup,

ROXALANA DRUSE IS DEAD.

The last act in a tragedy, which has attracted the attention of the entire

"Roxalana Druse is dead" reads the terse caption under this sketch which appeared in a newspaper shortly after she was hanged in the courthouse yard at Herkimer. Her crime: Killing her husband. Her case aroused national attention and considerable comment by women's groups.

**Mistreated, Brutalized, Roxy
Solved Her Problem By
Killing Her Husband.
Was Justice Served In
Her Famous Trial?**

Newspaper sketches of Roxalana differed as can be plainly seen!

Comment from Sheriff Delavan L. Cook, top law officer of Herkimer County, in the case of The State of New York versus Roxalana Druse, was succinct, all encompassing.

It was very much to the point.

Said that worthy in his written report:

"I did, on the 28th of February, 1887, between the hours of 10 o'clock in the forenoon and 4 o'clock in the afternoon, within a yard or enclosure adjoining the prison of the City of Herkimer, hang Roxalana Druse by the neck until she was dead."

A gaping crowd of the morbidly curious, as well as seventeen legally appointed witnesses attested to the accuracy of Sheriff Cook. The seventeen so stated by their signatures.

Mrs. Druse, described as a slightly built, somewhat frail woman, was arrested, tried and convicted of what was described in newspapers of that long past day of "perpetrating a horrible crime" on December 18, 1885, a mere seven days before Christmas.

Specifically she was convicted of placing a revolver's muzzle under the ear of an unsuspecting William Druse, her husband, and pulling the trigger. The revolver used was a pearl-handled, seven-chambered .22 caliber weapon, worth $2.95 when purchased.

The victim, who did not enjoy the comforts of the same bed with his wife, had roused himself from sleep shortly before and was eating breakfast. He obviously did not expect a bullet to be included in the menu of tea and herring and fell partially off his chair following the interruption. A rope was placed over his head and he was dragged to the floor. Mrs. Druse thereupon tried to fire more bullets into his body but could not work the trigger.

A problem thereupon developed as it usually does when such unique incidents occur. What to do with the body? The problem was solved when the surviving spouse used an axe to dismember the corpse and later tried to burn the remains in the living room stove. Mrs. Druse, according to one bit of testimony in her trial, removed her husband's head first, performing her individualistic surgery in the parlor.

The ashes and unburned portions were deposited in a nearby swamp, where they were later found.

The statement made by Sheriff Cook may have been the end of Roxalana but it did not bury the murder for it has lived in story and verse for the past ninety-five years. And when the century mark rolls around it probably will continue to be discussed.

There would be reason.

For one thing, the hanging of Mrs. Druse was considered the last legal hanging of a woman in New York State — and it is believed by some it might have been the last in the country.

At the time she mounted the gallows in the courthouse yard a state commission was seeking a "more humane method" of inflicting the death penalty, a penalty which had been administered to seven other women since earlier Colonial days.

The commission reported in January, 1888 that "protest and public excitement at the time of the Herkimer hanging showed the existence of widespread and deep-seated sentiment against the hanging of women." The report did not call for elimination of capital punishment but did call for substitution of the electric chair for the noose.

Another reason the murder will continue to be recalled is that the jury which decreed that she leave her unhappy life was all male and, noting this equally unhappy fact, women's groups protested vociferously.

Mail flowed to Governor David B. Hill in Albany, asking that he commute the sentence; the case had attracted nationwide attention and letters and petitions arrived from over the entire nation. One petition said:

"Public policy requires that brutal men should be made to know that if their brutality recoils upon themselves the Law will not exact the last drop of blood from their defenseless victims. Those victims have no vote, no home, no refuge, no one on the bench or among the jury who can regard, nor even understand, the plea their sufferings make for them."

There were appeals made and delays occurred in imposition of the sentence but the scene on the scaffold proved all attempts had been useless. Even while Roxalana sat on her rocking chair in her whitewashed cell, knitting the time away, an effort was made in the New York State legislature to pass a law which would exempt women from the death penalty. This chivalrous gesture, however, died in committee a few days before Mrs. Druse was jerked into the air by a heavy counterweight and remained suspended until declared officially dead.

The day that Mr. Druse met his fate had begun harshly. There had been argument. It is believed Mrs. Druse acted mostly on impulse; that the spark which set her off was based on past resentments based, in turn, upon brutal treatment and degradation of her person by the husband.

William was not the best of spouses. According to his self-made widow he was sixteen years older than she and therefore there existed a sizeable gap in ages. Furthermore, she described him as a "very odd genius" who not only had halitosis but read a great deal. Sympathetic neighbors confirmed that his language was not of the best and that he worked on Sundays. In one interview given by the widow, she said:

"My advise is never to get married. He was 38 and I was 22. I think it is rather a poor plan — it is a dreadful step to take and it ought to have more consideration than people give to it."

Roxalana trod the marriage route twice. Her first husband had left her widowed. He died naturally.

Testimony by the defense during her trial revealed that William had an explosive temper and had often threatened his wife physically. At one time he chased her around the house, threatening to cut her throat with a knife. Before he sat down to his last breakfast of tea and herring he had chased her with an axe, spitting out vituperation. Hardly a scene of domestic contentment.

At the time when violence visited the rundown Druse homestead, the wife was forty-four years of age, looked older. The conditions surrounding the family were materially miserable. Druse did as little work about the small farm as possible, kept the property going on a poverty level. He often complained when his wife spent a few dollars on household necessities.

The couple was not alone when the shooting occurred. Also present at the carnage were the children, Mary, nineteen, and George, nine, and a fourteen-year-old neighbor's son, a visitor.

Roxalana, or "Roxy" as she was often referred to, had Mary by her first husband and George, of course, by her unadored William. Mary was indicted as an accomplice but her mother stood trial alone. The daughter did testify for the mother's defense, which was based on justifiable homicide. Mary pleaded guilty to a charge of murder second degree and was sentenced to Onondaga Penitentiary for life. She was later pardoned.

The Herkimer Democrat on October 21, 1885 in a story quoted Mary after being jailed:

"I did not have any hand in the murder, although I was present. My mother was justified in what she did, as my father used her very brutally; sometimes he beat her with his fists and a club.

"I do not deserve to be sent here and I would not have pleaded guilty to murder in the second degree, only my lawyer told me I had better."

For a brief time Mary, at her request, remained with her mother in the Herkimer County jail before being removed to the Onondaga facility.

The inquest of the Druse killing was held in February, 1885. Mrs. Druse was indicted by a Herkimer County grand jury on April 16, and her trial began September 21. It was a short one. The verdict of guilty was given October 3 after a mere five hours of deliberation and sentencing three days later.

The death scene at N. Main and Church Streets in Herkimer, the old building which contained the jail in which Roxalana was incarcerated, and which adjoined the yard in which the gallows which took her life was located. The yard was located to the rear of the building, visible at photo's right.

The verdict, incidentally, was voiced shortly after midnight Sunday morning and this was cause to toll the bell on the courthouse. The sentence was given Tuesday morning before a packed courtroom. It was standing room only; folks had come from miles around, and the judge's remarks were described as "very touching," but they were devastating nevertheless. Mrs. Druse "sunk into her chair and was deeply affected." Following the voice of doom she was conducted from the courtroom assisted by two officers "and she seemed quite broken down."

Her counsel said he would apply for a new trial.

She was placed in a cell and remained there until all attempts came to naught. Her last view of the world was of the crowd which came to witness her fate and among the audience, if one might call it that, were seventeen witnesses appointed by the court who signed their names attesting to the fact that the ghastly sentence was carried out.

In the same building which held Mrs. Druse there was a strange assortment of individuals who faced trials for their alleged crimes. One was a physician who was accused of shooting a teacher. Another was an individual accused of killing his father-in-law. In another cell was a "pugilist" jailed for burglary, a man portrayed as a "brutish looking fellow, with the top of his head running down to his eyebrows."

Elsewhere in the jail a visiting reporter heard an "orchestra" which he traced to the cell containing four men, two of them accused of killing a railroad track hand during a riot in the southern portion of the county. One was playing an accordian, while another, minus a leg, "was rasping his gums with a mouth organ."

The reporter's comment:

"Between the two they produced a noise which the pen of man cannot describe!"

Prison officials did have the courtesy of separating the cell of Mrs. Druse from the rest of the prison by a partition which assured her of much desired privacy.

Roxalana in a conversation with prison officials, said she preferred hanging to life imprisonment — a wish subsequently duly granted.

In reviewing the famous case, one is apt to wonder. Was justice served?

The daughter Mary said in her defense of her mother that at one time her father had struck Roxalana with a horse whip and paid a neighbor five dollars to keep the incident quiet. Two other times, she said, he struck her with a club and placed a cord around her neck, threatening to choke her to death. And, of course, she related the happenings before the death breakfast, saying that her father, before setting down to his early meal of tea and herring, chased Roxalana with an axe and threatened to cut her throat with a knife because he was upset with the tea!

Was this woman punished too harshly? She seemed a captive to a life of poverty and degradation, living as she did, with a man unpredictable in mind and action. How much could any person take under such circumstances and retain sanity, let alone peace of mind?

The jury spoke and its decision was death. She walked to a gallows which had ten notches carved on it. What would be your decision?

* * * * * *

The writer calls attention to this interesting aspect: That while Roxalana was the last of her sex to be hanged in New York State and possibly the nation, others had suffered a similar fate in previous years.

In Clinton County, in 1825, for example, Peggy Facto became the first woman to be executed in that county. Her conviction was based upon an allegation she strangled her newborn daughter with a two-foot cord on September 5, 1824. She was hanged the day after a St. Patrick's Day celebration in Plattsburgh, on a gallows erected on a lot on Broad Street, where a school now stands. Peggy had an unusual escort, consisting of one rifle unit and one infantry unit of the United States Army.

Like the Roxalana hanging, the final period of Peggy Facto attracted hordes of the curious, including many women. She, too, had tried to eliminate evidence of her crime by burning the infant's body in a fireplace.

Following her death, the crowd dispersed. Many made for taverns. One group which had walked across the frozen surface of Lake Champlain from Grande Isle found itself inconvenienced. They had to return by boat.

The warm day of the hanging caused the ice to break up.

A curious aspect of this case rests in this: That a male "lover" of Peggy was reportedly at the scene of the crime and was charged with assisting the woman in the murder. He was acquitted. Seemingly both public opinion and the courts were far more charitable to the male than the female in such cases.

The Great Adirondack Fizzle

For A Brief Time There Was Dream
Of Foreign Empire In The
Mountains, But The Dream Collapsed
And Was Replaced By A
Hunting Camp

A fellow politician once described the gentleman as "mild, supine and luxurious." Hardly flattering.

His brother once despairingly wrote: "His behavior has never ceased bringing misfortune upon my Army; it is time to make an end of it."

He was kicked out of Spain and came to America to create an empire in the Northwestern Adirondack region.

He paid for his land with diamonds but they did not prove his best friend.

He never made it in the North Country.

* * * * * *

He was Joseph Bonaparte, and if the name sounds familiar, it should. He was Napoleon's older brother. After his Adirondack misadventure, he returned to Europe and eventually passed from the worldly scene in Florence, Italy, July 28, 1844, at age 76.

His role was not a role of dominance in history.

But history is a field in which one may conjecture. Had he succeeded in the creation of an industrial empire in the wilderness of those years long gone, the name of Bonaparte might have lived in splendor and glory in the United States today. As it is, there are few traces of his impact.

Lake Bonaparte, for one, in Lewis County, carries that name simply because at one time Joseph owned it, lock, stock, fish and barrel. On the map of the motorist today there is a small community called Bonaparte. It glitters not with the sound and sight of marching troops. On other maps there are North and South Bonaparte Roads, and a Bonaparte Creek, which runs through Camp Drum in adjacent Jefferson County.

And that's about it. No humming factories. No Bonaparte mines sunk into a region famous for its minerals. No regal castles. No magnificent palaces. Not even a clapboard Versailles. Nothing left of the dream which collapsed — a dream which some feel might have materialized in the arrival not only of Prince Joseph but, astonishingly, of Napoleon himself, since the Little Corporal upon loss of his power, had expressed interest in coming to America.

Joseph came into this world one year ahead of Napoleon, on January 7, 1768, at Corte, Corsica. Napoleon was born August 15, 1769, at Ajaccio, Corsica. The older brother studied law at the only

location on the globe where a weakened foundation gained world-wide fame — Pisa. After leaving Corsica, he settled in Marseilles and during his brother's more violent years, accompanied him on the Italian campaign.

Without Napoleon, Joseph might well have been swallowed in the anonymity of history.

Napoleon proclaimed Joseph King of Naples by decree on March 30, 1806, while keeping Joseph's claim as heir to the throne of France "open." Joseph's job in Naples was to "expel the Bourbon dynasty." He shone briefly; during his tenure as an appointed monarch he managed to abolish the remnants of what feudalism remained; reformed monastic orders, and reorganized the judicial, financial and education systems. Obviously with help.

In May, 1808, Napoleon presented Joseph with another gift, the Spanish throne, crown and along with these possessions, the opportunity to increase his bank account, which he did. This was accomplished despite the rough times which followed his appointment, and Joseph reigned only a few years. He was disliked by the Spaniards and pressures mounted to such an extent that he offered to abdicate at least four times.

The Duke of Wellington finally drove him out of Spain and Napoleon, after Joseph's hasty flight in 1813, wrote:

"His behavior has never ceased bringing misfortune upon my Army; it is time to make an end of it."

Napoleon lost his job as emperor April 11, 1814, was sent to Elba, from which he returned to take up arms once again. He was defeated at Waterloo June 18, 1815; was promptly deported to the island of St. Helena, a British possession, between South America and Africa in

There was great facial resemblance between Napoleon, left, and his brother Jospeh Bonaparte, right, as can be noted, but the resemblance ended there. Joseph, the older, ran his life pretty much on the coattails of his more prominent brother. He did participate in battle, but his accomplishments were dimly noted in history.

the South Atlantic. Here he died from cancer on May 5, 1821. (Some disagree, say he was poisoned.)

Reportedly Joseph, despite past differences with his brother, who had been declared an outlaw in Europe, offered to take his place as a prisoner to allow Napoleon to travel to the United States. The offer was refused. The Little Corporal found himself impatiently pacing St. Helena instead.

Joseph, in the meantime, had decided to set up a French empire in America, possibly one that might rival England in industry if not area. He had visions of establishing factories in and around the Black River Valley, of developing a domain with his brother at his side.

The area chosen: Northern Lewis County, a sparsely settled wilderness region where panthers and timber wolves roamed. This was a section of the Adirondacks where James Donatien Le Ray de Chaumont, a French businessman, owned large land holdings, including more than 30,000 acres in Franklin County, almost 74,000 acres in St. Lawrence County, 100,000 acres in Lewis, and more than 140,000 acres in Jefferson County. The region was popular with many French emigres who fled the French Revolution and the guillotine in 1789. The latter instrument, incidentally, an invention of Dr. J.I. Guillotin, was widely used during the Revolution as a

"more humane" way of separating a person from his or her head, and thus life.

A thought must interpose itself at this point: Had Napoleon himself managed to escape to America, can one imagine the military genius who commanded a half million conscripts in the invasion of Russia, working in the Adirondacks as a plant manager?

The very thought boggles the mind!

The purchase by Joseph of what he may have considered the "promised land" must have created an interesting scene. De Chaumont, whose company catered to wealthy buyers, was at his estate in Tourraine in 1815 when he was told that Joseph had arrived at Blois. De Chaumont had known Bonaparte for several years; was his guest at Mortefontaine when the treaty of September 30, 1800, was signed between the United States and France; the year before, Napoleon had ordered cessation of French raids on American shipping.

De Chaumont visited Blois, was invited to dine and at this time discussion centered on the proposed American pilgrimage to riches and power. Joseph is reported as saying:

"Well I remember you spoke to me formerly of your great possessions in the United States. If you have them still, I should like very much to have some in exchange

for a part of that silver I have there in those wagons, and which may be pillaged at any moment.

"Take four or five hundred thousand francs and give the equivalent in land."

De Chaumont knew the lands. The prince did not. Reluctantly he told Joseph it would not be in his best interest to complete a bargain, "where one party alone knew what it was about."

It made no difference.

Bonaparte replied:

"Oh! I know you well and I rely more upon your word than my own judgement."

Discussion continued. Joseph persisted. He repeatedly expressed trust. Finally De Chaumont said he would accept 400,000 francs and would give the prince a letter to give to his son, then in America, to complete the transaction. But he was still not convinced Bonaparte would continue to favor the deal; generously offered to refund the money if Bonaparte decided to withdraw.

In this fashion, Joseph became the owner of more than 150,000 acres of land and waters and forest, and reportedly promised payment in "certain diamonds" brought from Spain (along with, presumably, the silver) and in real estate.

The gem market, however, took a deep dip and diamonds fell to half their former price, and in 1820, Bonaparte agreed to accept approximately 26,000 acres for what was described as a "nominal payment" of $40,000.

De Chaumont's comment was gracious. He complimented the prince "upon his taste in selecting a tract abounding with picturesque landscapes, whose remote and extensive forests affording retreat to game, would enable him to establish a great hunting ground; qualities of soil, and fitness for settlers were only secondary considerations. He regrets, notwithstanding, that thus far, he has been unable to find among the 26,000 acres of land, a plateau of 200 acres to build his house upon, but he intends to keep up his researches this summer."

Bonaparte, incidentally, was authorized on March 31, 1825, to hold lands in New York State without the promise to become a citizen or expectation to become one. In his memoirs, the prince noted that Pennsylvania and other states did, indeed, allow aliens to possess lands.

What the tax situation was is not known. One doubts it was any kind of obstacle.

In America, Joseph did not carry the Bonaparte name. He was known as the Count de Survilliers. He reportedly first came to see his property about 1818. Then, ten years later, he arrived to "explore" them more fully, arriving by way of Albany. He enjoyed a stopover in Saratoga Springs, which community impressed him. From Saratoga it was westward and northward by coach and boat.

He had become acquainted "intimately" with the delights of social life in Saratoga by this time and was a much sought-after person in that developing community. It was at Saratoga he learned of Napoleon's death. Whether it dampened his spirits is not known, but by this time, his dreams of creating an empire were vanishing. He had abandoned that idea after having seen the difficulties which lay ahead in smothering a wilderness to create settlements. The idea of becoming a foreign power within the state may also have been dulled by outright opposition.

He did, however, direct roads to be cut; he did have a log house built at Lake Bonaparte; he also had constructed a frame house at the lake's outlet on 30 cleared acres, along with an ice house, sanitary facilities in the form of outhouses, and other useful buildings.

And he did order the erection of a log home at Natural Bridge on the Indian River, not to be confused with the river of the same name in Hamilton County, which serves as an outlet for both Indian and Abenaki Lakes.

Evidence of his influence in Lewis County was apparent. The Town of Diana was named just that at his request; the town was officially formed on April 26, 1830. Joseph had reason to choose the name, since Diana represented the goddess of the chase, chastity and the moon, and Bonaparte, a hunter, enjoyed pursuit of the first, elimination on occasion of the second, and as a lover of things beautiful, appreciated the third.

Furthermore, Diana was given not only a bow and arrows by her father, Jupiter, top god of the Romans, but a train of 60 nymphs, the latter entourage consisting of lesser goddesses of great beauty who lived in rivers, trees, mountains, valleys and dry caves, typical Adirondack country.

Beauty of face and figure was something the prince could and did appreciate and enjoy. Although he did have a wife in France, he managed never to avoid feminine companionship in America if he could help it, and reportedly sired daughters with a cooperative lady from Philadelphia, not the one in upstate New York, but in Pennsylvania.

Joseph possessed an American base, at Bordentown, New Jersey, where he owned an estate. It was here he kept his jewels and other properties, valued in the millions of francs. And it was here that some of his wealth, once buried in a garden in France, was shipped through efforts of a friend. Here too, was his art collection, which included creations by Raphael, Rubens, Titian and da Vinci — sold after his death to private collectors and museums throughout the world.

The New Jersey estate offered nothing in the way of hunting and during his brief periods of occupancy in Lewis County he found much to his liking. At this time the county was inhabited by species extinct today, including the timber wolf and the panther, or mountain lion. There were also moose, elk, black bear and white-tail deer. In those days there also would have been Canada lynx and the wolverine. In the 1830's, as a matter of interest, bounties of $5 were posted for the wolf or panther, and the price was raised to $10 in later years. Even foxes were not immune; they brought $1 each.

The author makes — and understandably so — no claim to the "authenticity" of the above creation. By a wide stretch of the imagination, however, the scene may represent what Napoleon might have become if he had acquiesced when his brother suggested he come to America. Napoleon, who loved the finer things in life, might well have become a local Adirondack merchant, specializing in an inventory closely tied to gracious living. Since the very thought is mind boggling, the scene above was the natural outgrowth.

The periods of visitation to his northern holdings were comparatively brief, a few weeks at a time. He did not live in what might be called primitive fashion, however. Here, in the wilderness, he enjoyed the company of "chosen companions, some of whom had witnessed and shared the sunny fortunes of the ex-king of Naples and Spain." Some of the social affairs must have shone with the same glitter of those held in more royal surroundings in France.

He traveled northward in a style of splendor, moving by colorful coach pulled by a team of six horses, accompanied by servants and other attendants.

One of them was Joseph Fortune, a veteran of Austerlitz, in which battle he lost his left hand. He acted as Bonaparte's armorer while at Lake Bonaparte; when the prince departed for France, Fortune remained, settled at Hermon, St. Lawrence County, where he became a respected gunsmith. He was truly an expert despite his handicap. He compensated for the loss of his hand by using a vise strapped to the stub of his wrist.

Bonaparte's trips must have been marvels to behold and unquestionably natives who beheld were amazed. It was not unusual for the caravan to stop on a dirt road, say between Evans Mills and Natural Bridge, in the midst of wilderness, for lunch, prepared on the spot and served on plates of gold in "regal ceremonies," by properly costumed servants. How such forest pests as the black fly and the mosquito were conquered is not a matter of record. Whether there was music other than that furnished by birds also is not recorded. Along with the coach and other vehicles was a wagon upon which a gondola was securely lashed. The craft, a six-oar job, served the ex-king on Lake Bonaparte.

Part of the route traveled on occasion by Bonaparte, is now part of Route 3. Joseph at least left that small legacy, but not in concrete or macadam.

Joseph returned to France about 1837. His lands moved into other hands.

His death in 1844, in a land strange to his beloved France, was a climax of many failures.

He never ascended the French throne.

He never did create an industrial empire in the Adirondacks.

And, of course, he never succeeded in creating anything save a passing episode in a region filled with unusual episodes, none of which, however, quite contained the potential which existed for so short a time.

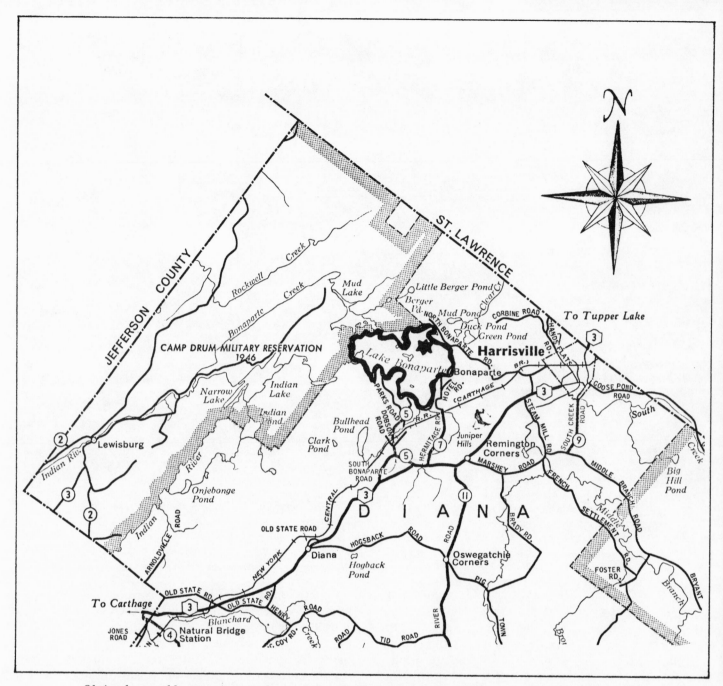

Obviously an old map, since it shows a New York Central Railroad line from Natural Bridge to the Harrisville area. It is of the Town of Diana and Lake Bonaparte is accentuated by heavy lines. Here Joseph Bonaparte hunted — and played. Note abundance of Bonaparte names in the township which Jospeh named.

A Tribute

Harold Hochschild, founder of the Adirondack Museum at Blue Mt. Lake, pictured in a relaxed pose in the area where he spent his summers. Chief supporter of the museum for a quarter century, Mr. Hochschild died in New York City January 23, 1981.

A man can be remembered for many things.

Harold K. Hochschild, founder of the prestigious Adirondack Museum at Blue Mt. Lake, who died January 23, 1981, was such a gentleman.

I remember him not only for his part in the creation of one of the finest museums in the country, but for a purely personal reason which may not be important to many but which was of great importance to me.

Hochschild, whose career was filled with many civic activities, was asked by Gov. Nelson A. Rockefeller in 1968 to assume the chairmanship of the Temporary Study Commission on the Future of the Adirondacks which, upon completion of its existence, called for the establishment of the Adirondack Park Agency now headquartered at Ray Brook.

In 1970 he held a press conference – with lunch – in a bank building in downtown Albany. I was among those invited. I had never met him; had a great desire to do so. But unforseen circumstances made it impossible for me to reach the meeting at noon. When this happens I usually make a telephone call. In this case I followed custom.

I reached the scene a half hour late.

To my amazement, he had held up not only the meeting but the luncheon! I was confronted with some rather disconcerting glares from members of the press associations and newspapers but was put at ease by the chairman and the meeting and luncheon went on.

I am sure Mr. Hochschild would have extended the same courtesy to others attending the meeting. But I was the person involved. One does not forget such an incident.

* * * * * *

His work completed as chairman, this remarkable man submitted his commission's two-volume report in December, 1970, and the recommendations called for the creation of the APA and the development of master plans governing state-owned and privately-owned lands in the six million acre Adirondack Park. They were approved by the legislature and Gov. Rockefeller promptly signed the bill into law.

I am sure that Gov. Rockefeller was offered a good deal of advice from Laurance, his brother, a noted conservationist in his own right, Laurance has been credited with offering the idea of making the Adirondack Park into a national one but the idea, offered in earlier years, died a quick death when protests were raised state-wide. All this, however, is beside the point; the Temporary Study Commission needed a strong hand. Hochschild was chosen.

The word remarkable is used in the description of the chairman.

It fits Harold Hochschild.

Born in New York City in 1892, he graduated from Yale University in 1912. Stocky and powerful in physique, he rated high as a collegiate boxer and swim-

mer. In the Adirondacks he was capable of swimming the length of the Eckford Chain of Lakes and in later years, until well into his eighties, he swam a half mile daily in Eagle Lake, weather permitting.

He entered the family's business, American Metal Company, in 1913; lived in China for approximately two years and in 1957 retired as chairman of the board of what by then had become the American Metal Company, then American Metal Climax, and which currently is the Amax Corporation.

Possessed of an astute business mind Hochschild also was gifted in language. He was a linquist; spoke several European languages and could converse in Russian and Mandarin Chinese. His ability in this field served him well when he enlisted in the United States Army during World War Two. Older than most he served in Army intelligence, in England and on the continent, where he assisted in interrogation of captured German officers. He held the rank of lieutenant colonel when he left the service.

Author of several volumes, on a variety of subjects, all pertaining to the region he loved, Hochschild's best known work is "Township 34," a 613-page historical study that has become a collector's item and a mainstay for historians. It has become a consistent shelf item in libraries.

His personal relationship with the Adirondacks began in 1904 upon his arrival at Blue Mt. Lake and that relationship climaxed in 1952 when he took the first steps leading to the opening of the Adirondack Museum to the public in 1957.

The early days started slowly. According to Craig Gilborn, director since 1972, "the museum's success, measured by a thirty-five percent rate of returnees among the nearly 1.5 million visitors who have come to the museum, has been due to Hochschild's ability to elicit the best that talented, skilled people have to offer."

The complex, which overlooks Blue Mt. Lake, and which is open from mid-June to mid-October, has become a research center as well as a museum. Its collection of historical data mounts steadily; writers have been accommodated from throughout the world.

In the words of Richard W. Lawrence of Elizabethtown, a former commissioner of the APA and later its first chairman:

"Harold Hochschild's most important contribution to New York State may have been the steadying and purposeful influence which he imparted to the Temporary Study Commission. He assumed leadership at a critical point when the commission was in serious disarray and in danger of bringing in half-hearted recommendations to solve the critical problems facing the vast Adirondack region.

"The commission was reorganized, was granted an extension of time to complete its studies and produce recommendations. The completed studies and final report have been hailed as unique landmarks in land-use planning."

In commenting on the pattern of Hochschild's life in the mountains, close friends had this to say:

"Mr. Hochschild's home at Eagle Nest, which he shared with his sister Gertrude Sergievsky and his brother Walter, was filled with friends who were united by their fondness for him and his wife, Mary Marquand Hochschild. Distinguished figures from public life hobnobbed in flannel shirts and blue jeans alongside of similarly attired teenagers and young adults embarked on careers in the theater, the environment or one of the professions. Mrs. Hochschild, who died in 1974, was a gifted gardener. The flower beds and plantings at the Adirondack Museum were developed under her direction."

In 1970 the museum received an award from Gov. Rockefeller for its "outstanding contribution to the artistic enhancement of New York State." In 1979 Mr. Hochschild received the James E. Allen Memorial Award for Distinguished Service to Education from the State Board of Regents.

He held honorary degrees from Hamilton College and Yale, St. Lawrence and Princeton Universities. He was on the board of several charitable and educational institutions, including the Correctional Association of New York, New York State Historical Association, the Valeria Home and the Institute of Advanced Studies, Princeton. For six years he was chairman of the African-American Institute, which seeks improvements in relations with Africa — a continent which Hochschild knew well from earlier visits on mining business. In addition, he served as President of the board of the Adirondack Historical Association, which is the administrative organization for the museum.

It was in 1960 that Mr. Hochschild was appointed chairman of the Committee on Museum Resources by the State Board of Regents.

The monument to Harold Hochschild, creator, innovator, businessman and philanthropist, rests in the nineteen exhibit buildings which make up the museum itself. In honoring the mountains the man is now honored, in return, by those who come to see and enjoy what he labored so mightily to accomplish.

ADIRONDACK MUSEUM
PHOTOS, FOLLOWING PAGES

The art displays at the Adirondack Museum are known throughout the nation; above is a reproduction of one. As in all instances where reproduction is in black and white, the sheer beauty of color is lacking; even though the drama of the moment remains.

One of the many dioramas which can be seen at the Adirondack Museum — not only seen, but described on a recording. Scene represents the felling of a tree, either spruce or white pine (center figures).

Another popular display in the Adirondack Museum, this one of a guide of yesteryear using a yoke to carry a guide boat. The museum features several boat displays, including early powered craft.

1935

FIRE TOWER.
THE SECOND FOREST FIRE TOWER IN THE ADIRONDACKS. ERECTED 1909. ONE OF 58 NOW MAINTAINED BY THE STATE IN ADIRONDACKS AND CATSKILLS.

NEW YORK STATE EDUCATION AND

Photo self explanatory as to what it represents. The tower, once manned by a fire observer, was saved from destruction through efforts of the Adirondack Museum and now remains as a permanent exhibit at the complex.

Ira Gray - Adirondack Woodsman

There is beauty in the following:

"I love to hear water running over stones, a woman with a low voice singing, a loon on a moonlit night, a partridge drumming in the fall, a hound dog after a rabbit, a robin just before a storm."

The words of a poet put to prose.

These are the words of Ira Gray, affectionately known to thousands of North Country residents and travelers as "Adirondack Ike," who died in the Glens Falls Hospital Sunday, August 1, 1982, at the age of 95. Quietly, as he lived.

Gray, one of the last of the great Adirondack woodsmen, a former guide, a hunter of note, a born naturalist who felt strongly enough about the environment in which he lived to place his thoughts on paper, is memorialized in a small museum at Northville, Fulton County, along the Sacandaga Reservoir, where his memorabilia is now kept.

The museum was constructed by a friend, Paul Bradt, Northville contractor and is open to the public Monday through Saturday during the summer and Monday through Friday in other months.

Ira's friends were legion in number and one who wrote feelingly and in depth about him in 1977, when Ira became 90, is Robert F. Hall, former publisher of the Warrensburg News and more recently retired as editor of the New York State Conservationist Magazine. Mr. Hall lives in Willsboro; continues his interest in things Adirondack, and during June, 1982, chaired a committee celebrating the start of construction of a fish ladder for salmon, the first such in New York State. The ladder, instituted through the efforts of Larry Strait, EnCon biologist, and helped in the legislature by Senator Ronald Stafford and Assemblyman Andrew Ryan (appropriation of funds needed), has been constructed by Laquidara, Inc., a Ballston Spa general contracting firm.

It enables spawning landlocked salmon to surmount a dam at Willsboro in the Boquet River.

The writer is indebted to two individuals for this chapter, Bob Hall and Charles Hawley of Lake George Village, Chairman of the Lake George Park Commission and a well known Adirondack artist, whose oil portraits are reproduced.

Hall's comments:

* * * * * *

The Adirondack region is known for two unique products, the Adirondack guideboat and the Adirondack guide.

In the latter distinguished company is Ira Gray who celebrated his 90th birthday in October and who has spent most of those 90 years in Brooks Bay near Corinth. Born in 1886 his life spans a period of upstate history in which the way of life was peculiarly primitive in that remote communities did not share the conveniences which technology and Mr. Edison's inventions were bringing to more populous areas.

But Ira, known widely as Ike, continued the primitive style of living and working through choice, because it enabled him to remain closer to nature, to the forests and streams and the wildlife essential to that peace of mind he so prized.

We know a great deal about Ike Gray from two sources. Somewhere along that active life, when he wasn't whittling figures of birds and animals from white pine, he was putting on paper his recollections of his own past which constitutes for us not only his personal history but an authentic record of how people lived. Our second source is the painting of Ira Gray by Charles Hawley, a well known Adirondack artist with what he calls "a strong emotional attachment to the *old* Adirondacks." A lifelong resident of Lake George whose family came there in the 1790's, Hawley was understandably attracted to Gray and Gray to him. Out of this friendship came the portrait reproduced here, communicating without sentimentality or idealizing the personality and character of the man.

As a youngster on his stepfather's farm, Ike Gray performed his chores through the seasons. He found his recreation with other farm boys in the swimming hole in summer; in autumn and winter he hunted rabbits and trapped beaver, and it must be admitted often shot woodchucks for sport.

His journal, published in 1975 and entitled "Follow My Moccasin Tracks," is dedicated to "the wild animals of the Adirondacks." He estimated that over the years he had killed four moose, three bear, hundreds of rabbits and 84 deer. Except for his boyhood zeal when he shot woodchucks to show off his markmanship, he killed only for food. He was in fact very critical of some fellow hunters. "I never could see any sport of hunting coon with dogs," he wrote. "Three or four men, two or three dogs after one little coon!"

He trapped for what was his only cash at times and his journal records that over the years he trapped 100 beaver, 38 foxes and "a couple of mink." During three nights in one spring, Ike's trap line yielded five beavers. "The two old ones brought $65 each and the three younger ones $45 each," he recalled.

Some cash came from guiding "sports" who came to the Adirondacks to hunt deer, but he wasn't impressed by their fat pocketbooks. Those were the days when it was permissible to hunt with dogs and Ike loved his deer hounds better than the generous offers to buy them made by the sports. He relates one incident which came near to a fist fight when a sport who had employed him got his kicks from torturing a wounded deer.

Ike could outwalk most people, an ability he learned from his stepfather. "Father walked from Hadley to Poughkeepsie and drove 42 yoke of oxen," he remembered. "The driver would go ahead with his horse and wagon and find a place to spend the night. . .Father got $1.25 a day and his carfare back to Hadley. He walked from Hadley home."

Ike and a pal walked the Northville-Lake Placid trail — 135 miles — in six days. He recalls walking to Harrisburg. "I got there at noon, 14 miles. I hunted that afternoon. I was guiding a party from Troy. We got a deer and a fox that afternoon."

The sounds, sights and smells of the woods inspired Ike and he expressed his delight: "I love to hear water running over stones, a woman with a low voice singing, a loon on a moonlit night, a partridge drumming in the fall, a hound dog after a rabbit, a robin just before a storm.

"I love to see sunrise and sunset when nice weather, snow or ice on trees, a small lake, a waterfall, a coon with her family, an otter with hers.

This is the oil painting referred to by Bob Hall in his fine article on Ira Gray. The painting was done by Charles Hawley of Lake George and was reprinted, with Hall's article, by the New York State Conservationist Magazine. Mr. Hall's story appeared in the same publication when he edited that magazine. Another painting by Mr. Hawley is reproduced on the following page.

"I love to feel a cool breeze on my face. I love to smell new plowed earth, balsam trees, a field of new mown hay. I love to taste maple sugar, cool milk."

He sums up his recollections with these words:

"I have really enjoyed my life and hope to continue doing so. I am in fair health, can still see good enough to shoot a rifle without glasses, have all my faculties What more can a man ask for?"

Ike represents an era nearing its end, but in the stories he put on paper and in his portrait painted by Hawley, something very valuable has been preserved for future generations that want to know about the region's past and its people.

Below: A photograph of Adirondack Ike taken in 1952 with Spot at his side. At right: Black and white reproduction does not bring out the full beauty of this portrait painted by Charles Hawley of Lake George, a close friend of Ira Gray, but even a black and white reproduction brings out in vivid detail the rugged features and the inner soul of the old mountain man. The hands, gnarled with arthritis, rest upon a walking stick; the look is pensive, as though Ira was gazing at a panorama which included all the years spent in the mountains he loved. Portrait painted in the late 1970's, now hangs on the wall at the Hawley home.

An Eagle Called Rehab

Rehab — before he was shot by an unknown person.
The white head of the bald eagle develops when maturity is reached, in about five years.

**"Three Times And Out" Meant
Nothing To This Eagle —
Once Again Flying High**

The American bald eagle officially became the symbol of nationhood on June 20, 1782.

The bird has had rough going ever since.

It has been hunted as a "killer" of livestock in the West, which is nonsense. It has died an agonizing death from eating poison bait put out to eliminate coyote predation. At one time a bounty of $50 a head was placed on the bird in Alaska, a bounty removed many years ago after loud public protest.

In Colonial days, the eagle was common in the Adirondacks. But its population diminished steadily as civilization moved "forward," cutting into its native habitat. To add to the tragedy, the pesticide known as DDT came into use and was absorbed by the food sources of the eagle, small game and fish. Ingestion of this chemical not only inhibited egg laying and hatching but caused females to lay soft-shelled eggs, easily broken.

The population continued downward. It is known that prior to the 1950's, New York State had approximately seventy nesting pairs, many of them soaring over the North Country. Others were located in western New York. Since 1960 and until 1980 there has been only one known active nest in the entire state and this was in the Finger Lakes region.

At rest and at unease is this bald eagle. Once exterminated from the Adirondacks, the balds seem to be returning; EnCon is proving a major help in the restocking program.

The irony, if one may call it that, rests in the fact that the national emblem of America's might was declared to be an endangered species in most states, and in those few where it has managed to survive, it has been considered a threatened species. It is now protected by federal and state laws.

It was in 1973 that New York State launched its own restoration project. In this program young eagles are obtained from other states and raised, or hacked, in this state. Phase 1 saw a hacking station at the Montezuma National Wildlife Refuge. In the interim years twenty-three bald eagles were raised and released.

Phase 2 began in 1981, will continue until 1985, and the plan calls for the hacking of one-hundred-and-twenty-nine eagles during that period. Oak Orchard Wildlife Management Area near Batavia was chosen as the second release site. In 1981 twenty-one eaglets were acquired from elsewhere, raised and released. Five are known to have died from electrocution (power wires), shootings and unknown causes. Another group of twenty-one was scheduled for 1982.

All of which brings us to the story of an eagle called Rehab, an immature, two-year-old bird which has had its share of misery. It is a story which hits home.

First, the name itself: Rehab is a shortening of "rehabilitation," and the reason the bird acquired that name will become obvious.

The story starts in May, 1982.

On or about May 11, almost 200 years to the day of the designation of the eagle as the national emblem, an unknown individual minus not only compassion but brains, aimed a shotgun at the bird and peppered its body with pellets. The location of the shooting is not known.

What is known is that Rehab eventually ended up in the Adirondack area of Jay, Essex County, near the covered bridge which spans the East Branch of the Ausable River.

It could have been shot one hundred miles distant from that spot. Or blasted fifty miles or less. The location is of no consequence at this point. What is is that the bird ended up in the Jay area, where it attracted notice.

It was sighted frequently. Hundreds heard of the bird and traveled for a look. It did not act normally. It appeared emaciated. When it did fly, it was done with difficulty. There were rumors it was being harassed by some. The rumors reached federal and state officials. They began an investigation which proved the bird had made a wise choise to visit Jay. What happened afterward is a tribute not only to area residents who cooperated but to investigating personnel. Nothing came of the rumors of harassment. Plenty of activity came shortly thereafter.

Special Agent Ed Whalen of the U.S. Fish and Wildlife Service's division of law enforcement arrived at the scene from Champlain, along with EnCon officials from the Jay area and Albany. All determined the eagle was indeed acting in a most unusual manner. Wildlife specialist Gary Will, for instance, was able to approach to within fifteen feet of the eagle before it showed agitation. Said Will:

"He was sitting on a branch, very attentive, very alert, but he showed no intention of flying as I approached."

A specialist from the wildlife laboratory in Delmar, near Albany, was called. Lois Marshall, who responded, also determined the bird was acting abnormally. The decision was made to capture it for examination.

Proof of illness became evident when the eagle allowed a blanket to be dropped over its body. It was then placed in a transport container and ended up at the office of an Albany area veterinarian, Dr. Edward Becker, who has often done rehabilitation work on casualties delivered by EnCon.

It was at this time the name Rehab was applied. The reason, as explained to me by Peter Nye, in charge of the endangered species unit of EnCon, was that the bird had suffered before. Shortly after birth in Minnesota, it fell from its nest, causing shock and damage to tail and wing feather growth. It recovered after treatment.

Then further misfortune; Rehab again fell out of a tree and suffered further feather breakage and damage. More treatment, and then release.

Then came the shooting. The sighting at Jay was the first since the eagle's release from the Oak Orchard site.

This writer talked to Dr. Becker shortly after he received the eagle. That gentleman, in examining Rehab, found eight shotgun pellets in the bird's body.

None had struck a vital organ. But there was damage to a wing, and Rehab was given a 50-50 chance of survival. The bird's chances of once again taking to the air were declared minimal. Rehab was indeed emaciated. During the latter portion of his days at Jay he was unable to catch food. He had lost several pounds. He was listless. Placed in a spacious, sheltered enclosure outside the veterinarian's office the bird slowly began recovery. His appetite picked up to an enormous extent; he was fed highway-killed squirrels, venison from carcasses brought to the Delmar lab and fish. He ate everything. Signs of improvement were notable.

Rehab remained at Dr. Becker's place for several weeks. He was then transferred to the Endangered Species unit at Delmar. It soon became evident the bird had regained not only strength but a desire to actually fly. Daily, in early morning, he was given a chance to prove his ability.

The end of a long cord was attached to one leg. The other end was attached to a light weight. Rehab was released by hand. He flew a short distance. Days went by. Each flight became longer. Finally the day came when the bird reached the full length of the cord. The weight stopped him; he landed without difficulty.

The process was repeated day after day.

And each day it became obvious that the eagle had not only surmounted all difficulties, but would once again reach the heights!

The pellets remained in his body. It was felt removal would endanger recovery. Obviously the decision was a wise one; the pellets interfered not one whit.

Rehab was fitted with a tiny transmitter, attached to tail feathers. Such remains for a limited time because natural loss of feathers means the transmitter will be lost as well. But while the device is in place the flight of a bird so equipped can be monitored.

Then came the day for release.

On August 4, the Plattsburgh-Republican carried a by-line story by David Clayton, staff writer. It was date-lined Jay. I quote:

"In the Year of the Eagle, on the day of his freedom, Rehab spread his wings and flew.

"Into the crisp, sunny morning flew the North Country's most celebrated bald eagle.

"There on a hillside facing the Sentinel and Wilmington Mountain ranges, 25 people shared a moment of marvelous silence as Rehab first fluttered, then spread his seven-foot wings and met the open air as a healthy eagle should — with beautiful, powerful flight.

The silence on that hillside in Jay was first broken by Wildlife biologist Gary Will.

" 'YaaHooo!' he screamed as Rehab disappeared over the treetops.

" 'Pretty neat, huh?' said Barbara Loucks, who has been working with Rehab these past few weeks at the Delmar Wildlife Refuge.

"Considering that Rehab still has eight shotgun pellets in him, it was pretty neat indeed.

"Miraculous, some say."

In the latter part of the month, this writer received information that Rehab had been sighted in an area near Lake Champlain. The function of defecation had been noted, and interpreted by observers, this meant the bird had reverted to the wild, that it was catching its own food and that the digestive processes were working as they should.

The flight pattern seemed to be directing the bird toward Vermont. Vermont wildlife authorities were notified.

If, between this writing and your reading, nothing untoward has occurred, Rehab is back where he belongs, soaring through blue skies, possibly eventually even seeking a mate to which he will be beholden for a long life. It is the fervent hope of all those concerned no further tragedy will mar his existence.

He has had quite enough.

Bigfoot At Indian Lake

The year was 1932.

The Great Depression had struck and its effect were still being felt. Perhaps that was one reason an unknown man took to the woods in the Indian Lake section of the Adirondacks were he proceeded to live in the wilderness in incredibly primitive fashion.

Perhaps there was another reason; the individual may have been "on the run" from the law. Whatever the purpose, his identity has never been solved. Nor have his motives.

His movements created a minor sensation, a topic of conversation, a period of fear.

At times in the March snows which lay over the forest floor his footprints measured almost two feet in length. Bigfoot? That was a name bandied about. The footprints showed no definite form; it was as though rounded bundles of cloth or fur had been inscribed in the snow.

The man's end came abruptly.

He was killed just over the Essex County line in an exchange of gun fire.

The story is a strange episode in mountain history; involves a great deal of territory since the stranger did much traveling. Always on foot, no matter the depth of snow. Never on snowshoes.

The story begins on the day he arrived in the woods, an entry made no one knows where, and at a time no one can figure out to this day. In February two trappers near Blue Mt. Lake took shelter in a cabin. During their occupancy they were startled to hear a slight noise outside the cabin window. Framed in that aperture was a face, showing little detail not only because of the night but because it was partially covered. When the intruder realized he was noticed, he promptly disappeared.

The tracks left were huge, baffling. What manner of man had left them?

Body of "Bigfoot" or the "Wildman," as some called him, rests on a toboggan after he was shot during gunfight.

The mystery grew, as did apprehension, as time went on. The strange imprints were seen in the Chain Lakes and other areas. Then sightings occurred, but observers saw the man from a distance, and details could not be ascertained. What was given was a description of a person seemingly wrapped in shaggy clothing, who bundled his feet in either rags or skins. A strange cape seemed to be wrapped about his shoulders. His weight was estimated at about one-hundred-and-fifty pounds; his height about six feet. When sighted he ran, throwing up clouds of snow as he vanished.

There came then reports of vandalism, of camps broken into, articles stolen. One report led to alarm; a lumber camp had been invaded and a shotgun, shells and a few dollars in Canadian money had been heisted. Reports followed that camps were being burned to the ground; one fire which destroyed a sawmill in Hamilton County was attributed to the arsonic tendencies of the unknown wanderer.

In more isolated areas residents became fearful enough to securely lock windows and doors.

Finally it was determined, after calls had come into the State Police and other law enforcement agencies, to try to locate the man, to effect capture or to offer help.

A search party was organized in early March. Tracks were found. Traveling on snowshoes the group found they led to an abandoned sawmill. As the party approached, a voice called out:

"Leave me alone!"

He was requested to leave the building.

The answer was a shotgun blast. One member of the search party fell but he found Providence on his side; a silver dollar he carried deflected the slug.

Gunfire was exchanged. Abruptly silence settled over the mill. Another call was made to surrender. There was no response. An approach was cautiously made.

Only a body greeted the party. The unknown lay flat on the cold floor; the shotgun at his side. He had been shot in the abdomen.

He resembled an apparition. It was obvious he had spent much time in the woods. His age was estimated at from twenty-five to thirty years. He wore a collection of old, torn clothing covered with untanned bear and deer hides. A cloth hood covered his head. His feet were still wrapped in huge bundles of skins, fresh, untanned deer skins. Remnants of venison were found; it was reported he killed and ate his food raw. Later, as the body was looked over closely, it was found he at one time had received a bullet wound in the head — apparently some years previously.

All efforts to identify him failed. He carried no papers. No individual of his description had been reported missing throughout the entire region.

His body was removed by toboggan from the mill area and carried to an undertaker. Records show he was buried in the North Creek area.

So it is claimed. And so ends another unusual happening in the North Country.

Following Pages:
A Reporter's Album

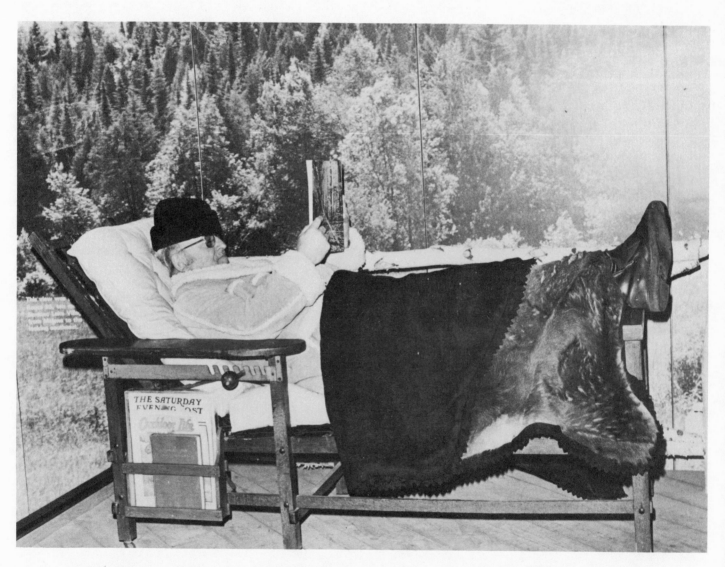

For easy reading the author recommends using this type of reclining chair, known as the " 'Rondack Recliner." But don't use it at the New York State Museum where the 19th century invention is exhibited. The photograph was taken after permission was obtained from museum authorities. The author is in what was known as the "Fowler" position, an actual description and one, it is felt, developed by a Dr. Fowler (no relation) for patients recovering from tuberculosis in the Saranac Lake area. Perhaps this reclining chair was the forerunner of the modern aluminum tubing furniture used during summer days. Could be.

Split Rock Falls on the Boquet River, south of Elizabethtown, Rt. 9, is now state property, the gift in 1982 of the Richard W. Lawrence family of that community. Photo above, used through courtesy of the State Commerce Department, shows series of pools, while sketch below shows cross-section. Pools are potholes, ground by swirling boulders during the ice age meltage. An iron forge was once located at base of the falls.

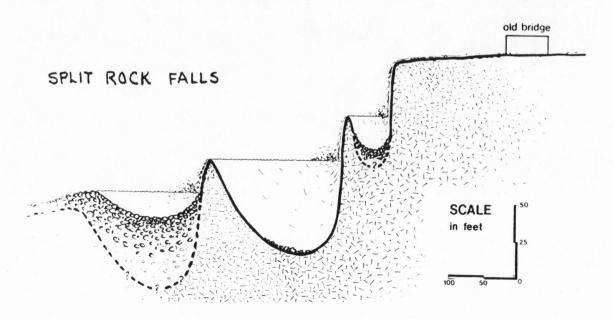

SPLIT ROCK FALLS

old bridge

SCALE
in feet

50

25

100   50   0

A scene along the Boquet, below Split Rock Falls, as the waters make their way to join Lake Champlain.

You'll never see this kind of display of bathing beauties unless the country returns to the Victorian era. Photo, used through courtesy of the Lake George Historical Society, illustrates the type of swimming wear worn at Lake George at the turn of the century. Bare arms and faces, obviously, were not considered indecent!

Below shows no bathing beauties, but depicts a camping scene in the Thousand Islands area. Note boats pulled on shore; today they would be worth thousands. They could have been Rushton made.

Mementos left behind. At right: This scythe was found by Tom Butler and Don Filkins as they snow-shoed in the North Creek area. As Tom said: "How many generations have come and gone since this relic was hung on a limb for perhaps a few minutes rest on a hot summer's day? Note that the cutting edge is completely overgrown within the tree itself and we found nails joining the wood to metal were four-sided, that is, square."

Lower photo: If trees can devour scythes, the same holds true for "eating" horseshoes! Years ago Jim Farrell of Indian Lake showed me this shoe, com-pletely enveloped within a tree. It was probably cast by an animal working a lumber tract in early days, and a 'jack found it, hung it on a limb. Nature did the rest.

Once, in ancient times, Big Nose Mt., at left, and Little Nose, at right, were joined, and over the ridge roared a waterfall greater than Niagara Falls. You are looking east from a point along Rt. 5S, several miles west of Amsterdam. The giant drop was part of the Iro-Mohawk, the river which drained the Great Lakes area and part of northern New York; it is believed the Cohoes Mastodon's carcass floated down this big stream and eventually bogged down in the pothole at Cohoes where it was found.

A portion of the Adirondacks drains into the St. Lawrence River; the "continental divide" is in the Blue Mt. Lake area. Hudson's River receives the rest. This is a scene at the Cohoes Falls on the Mohawk River, a Hudson tributary which during its course through the Mohawk Valley receives many Adirondack streams. When the early Dutch occupied the Albany area, they found beached whales at the "sprouts of the Mohawk," that is, the channels which carried the water from the falls into the Hudson. The monsters had negotiated the Hudson from the sea during a time of freshet.

No nimrod scouting for big game will ever see one of these monsters today and for good reason. The animal is a giant ground sloth, the size of an elephant. It existed during Pleistocene times. It is believed that the sloth, so tall that the head of which could peer into a modern day second story window, roamed the state at the time of the mammoth.

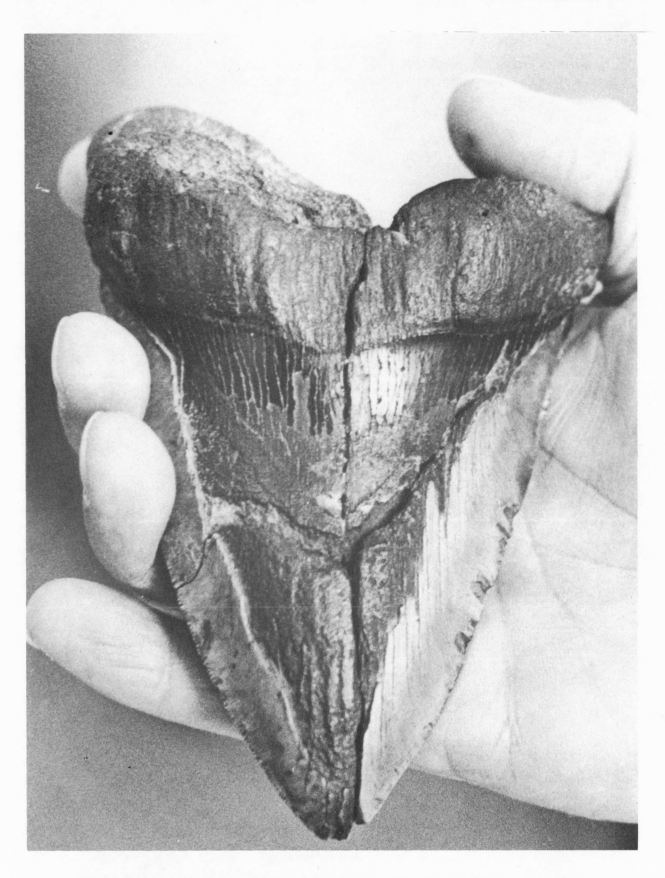

Shark's tooth found in a house purchased in Cohoes by Albert Ferris, section superintendent, Barge Canal, Waterford. Tooth is about four-and-one-half inches long, weighs 14-1/2 ounces! It is believed to have been found by a workman excavating the Cohoes Mastodon in the late 1800's, an animal found in a pothole created by the ancient Iro-Mohawk. Tooth is believed to be at least ten million years old and the possibility its owner swam in an inland sea which once covered much of the state is not discounted. If so, the creature must have run ninety to one hundred feet in length!

Albert Ferris, Section Superintendent, Barge Canal, Waterford, inspects the prehistoric shark's tooth he found in a home he purchased.

A side view of the shark's tooth found along the Mohawk.

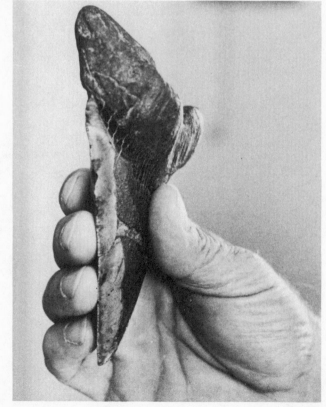

Canada Geese

Canada geese during an early stage of winter. While the Canadas migrate, some will remain while food supplies last. Sections of Lake Champlain are known as refugees for these familiar travelers whose V-shaped formations in flight create a most pleasant sight. Flight is not without danger, however, instances have been known of lightning kills.

It must be quite a sight to see thousands of Canada geese starting their southward flight from northern areas of the continent. They are in a period of molt, or shedding and growing new feathers, and walk, not fly, for the first fifty or so miles!

Two unusual residents of the woodlands: Flying squirrel at left, an animal which never received its "wings" from an academy, but was born with membranes between its legs. Spread, these allow it to glide from tree to tree. Seldom seen by the average traveler.

At right is a ground-based amphibian making its way through a perilous world minus a jumping leg. The creature was photographed in the Miami River area between Speculator and Indian Lake. It apparently lives with the philosophy that a half a jump is better than none.

Around the turn of the century it was estimated that the waters of LaChute, the outlet to Lake George, would furnish about "700 horsepower." The falls in this two-mile stretch of outlet has indeed been used by mills, although that is a thing of the past. Photo of the drop taken at Ticonderoga when the waters of Lake George were high. Lower photo denotes another form of horsepower, this measure of energy spotted using an Adirondack highway for a casual stroll. The horse is a welcome change from deer and an occasional bear.

North Country residents had much to say and demonstrate about before the gubernatorial primaries, particularly concerning Mayor Ed Koch's comments about the upstate area. This was one of the sights to see in the Schroon Lake Fourth of July parade in 1982. Seated are Mr. and Mrs. Paul Crear of Crear Farm, Severance. The cow pulling the rig is named Buttercup; pedigree name is Quicksilver Queen of Diamonds. She was a junior champ at the Essex County Fair. The Jersey is now seven years old; quick to learn, and proof is in the fact that Mrs. Crear trained her to the harness and command in only a few days! The second Jersey is Buttercup's niece. The name? Happy!

North Country's answer to a problem, symbolic of course, but very much to the point. Some years ago the state felt it did not have enough money in the budget to adequately operate the state skiing facilities at Gore Mt. at North Creek. An uproar developed and the money was found. But in the meantime, this "gallows" appeared overnight near North Creek. Rumor has it an effigy (of NYS) appeared, but was removed and when the photo was snapped, the noose was empty.

154

Many guides lived lonely lives during portions of the year when they weren't busy leading city "sports" to game and tending to campfire chores. It was not unusual for some to locate on state or private lands, building a cabin thereon. Typical is the guide's camp above. Most lived pretty much off the land.

Photo taken in the 1890's, on Fourth Lake, Fulton Chain of Lakes. No outboards in those days; the power was steam, not gasoline. The Adirondacks were awakening to the gold mine of the tourist and hunting trade.

HISTORIC NEW YORK
THE BLACK RIVER COUNTRY

As you look out from this vantage point, you see four locks of the old Black River Canal. These enclosures, with gates at either end, were used in raising or lowering boats as they passed from one level to another. Construction was a costly project since 109 locks were built along the 35 mile route. Completed in 1855, it served as a "feeder" for the Erie and later Barge Canal System. This Rome to Carthage waterway was instrumental in the opening of the "North Country." Grain and lumber were sent as far as Buffalo and New York City in exchange for clothing and machinery. As the canal building "fever" waned, the Black River section fell to disuse and was finally abandoned in 1926.

Today, this region is prime dairy country. The fine "sharp" cheese of this part of the Empire State ranks among the best in the world. It has been the winner at innumerable fairs and foreign competitions.

EDUCATION DEPARTMENT · STATE OF NEW YORK 1969 · DEPARTMENT OF TRANSPORTATION

Route 12, north of Utica, offers fine scenery — as well as this historical spot. The State Department of Transportation sign, above, is self explanatory. At left is a portion of the old canal gradually being taken over by growth.

New salmon fish ladder as it appears today on Boquet River at Willsboro. Fish enter aperture, (right center), swim up incline and enter river above dam. Note stairway at left, leading to windows through which salmon may be seen by spectators.

Photo of principals involved in ceremonies June 19, 1982, at Willsboro, celebrating the start of construction of the salmon ladder. Committee Chairman Robert F. Hall is at the microphone. Committee members included: Greg Garvey, Marcia Bierce, Nancy Hanks, Peter Casamento, Jack Cleary, Mike Dickerson, Kip Gariss, Livingston Hatch, Supervisor Florence Hathaway, Elwyn Hoke, Walter LaDuke, Mike McKenna, Lyman Mero, Mark McKenna and Martin Rosenkranz. Among speakers was Peter Lanahan, first deputy commissioner, EnCon, and Bill Roden, well known Adirondack outdoor columnist.

Above: Daniel S. Plosila, Supervising Aquatic Biologist, Lake Champlain Unit, EnCon, holds seven-pound male salmon tagged at Willsboro ladder. Lower left: Spectators watch for fish at windows. Lower right: Spillway leading to freedom above. Abrupt rise in rear is barrier to lamphrey eels; salmon leap the wier; the parasitic eels cannot.

An excellent photograph by Peter Brownsey, Rt. 7, Niskayuna, of Rockwell Falls in the winter. The drop is part of Hudson's River between Lake Luzerne and Hadley, was once the site of a mill. When this photo was snapped, the river was running fairly full. Photo is used for front and rear cover of this volume.

160

The D&H bridge spanning the Sacandaga River, near Lake Luzerne. The Sacandaga is near joining the Hudson. Bridge reputedly one of the oldest in the North Country. Photo taken by Peter Brownsey.

161

When the Upper Hudson and the Boreas River needed stocking with trout, the Johnsburg Fish and Game Club came to the rescue, helping EnCon workers. Scene above shows "bucket brigade" method of dumping trout into the Hudson, north of North River, along the D&H Railroad tracks. At left: The railroad furnished a small, automotive-type hauler, equipped with RR wheels, to pull a flatcar on which fish tanks were loaded. The late Homer Preston, Conservation Officer, often went along on the trips. Fish delivered from hatcheries, including the one at Warrensburg.

Efforts to restock the Adirondacks with elk were made in the early part of the 20th century but one by one the big animals disappeared; the last known elk was shot in the mountains in 1946 by a hunter who mistook it for a white-tail. Pictured is a band or "gang" of elk in the Little Tupper Lake region, obviously wintering well. It is believed most of the stock brought into the mountains fell before native hunters.

At right: Photo of elk, similar to those which once roamed the Adirondacks. Might they be restocked and live? Possibly. There are fifteen wilderness areas in the Park which prohibit motorized traffic which would give elk a breather from all save foot hunters.

163

During the winter of 1981-82, Speculator possessed one of the most unusual of snow-ice sculptures, created by Daniel Moran of Lake Pleasant, pictured above at the sled. Blocks of ice form background and platform. The dogs and sled were made in a most unusual way. Snow was collected in a tub and mixed with water. The resulting slush was built into what you see; Moran had to work fast because freezing temperatures hardened the slush quickly. Once the forms were created, a vegetable coloring was applied. The display made a tremendous impression and drew spectators from over the entire area.

Kindness holds no terror. Photo taken several years ago of Ernie Thompson, gate superintendent at the dam holding back the Stillwater Reservoir on the headwaters of the Beaver River, Herkimer County. The reservoir area holds one of the most unusual of communities, Beaver River Flow, surrounded entirely by Forest Preserve lands; it is accessible only by water.

The years have seen many unusual sights along the Champlain Canal. Here's one, recorded by the camera in August, 1952. The canal split the Charles Wright farm and to reach pasture cattle began swimming the canal in 1916. Photo shows a herd of Guernseys as it approaches the western side of the canal. Once the herd was driven miles to cross, but one day an adventurous bovine made the swim, and the practice was established. When the cattle swam, boaters were advised of the scene they might expect to encounter. Up to 1952, when the author photographed the swimmers, only one bovine mallard had been lost to drowning. Photo taken at Smith's Basin.

A sad (for the prisoners) scene at Clinton Prison, Dannemora, about 1874, when the convicts were lined up, hand on shoulder style, guarded by keepers, for benefit of the photographer, who happened to be Stoddard. Photo obtained through facilities of the Adirondack Museum at Blue Mt. Lake. Note striped uniforms worn by prisoners in those days.

Title is "Lost in a snowstorm." The gentleman may be lost, but he shows little knowledge, since he could well use the hatchet at his belt for shelter or fire — provided, of course, he had the matches to ignite the blaze. Reproduction of old painting.

Not the Boquet River and not the dam at Willsboro. This is a scene drawn by the noted artist Henry S. Watson and published in a report by the Forest, Fish and Game Commission around the turn of the century. It does denote, however, what scenes may be like when landlocked salmon fishing becomes a major activity at Willsboro when the fish ladder is put into full use.

The title to this old photo, taken during the late 1800's, was "Watching for another one." Note size of buck. Note also clothing worn, particularly the hunter, second from left, sporting a derby. Also note leggings on individuals at left and right, plus the wearer of the derby.

This would be illegal today — but it was not in the day when game existed in the mountains for the taking — and selling. Location of photo is not available. It was taken in late 1800's.

169

One of the most noted clergymen who roamed the Adirondacks was The Rev. Frank Reed, one time editor of a lumberman's publication, and more widely known as the author of "Lumberjack Skypilot." As such he traveled many miles on foot, on snowshoes if the need arose, to visit and minister to the spiritual needs of lumberjacks working in the deep wilderness. He was an exceptional man, a friend of the writer, and an encyclopedia when it came to matters pertaining to the mountains. He was widely known in the Old Forge and other areas.

An excellent photo of a pulp drive in the Adirondacks, stream unknown. Note ice in background, which still sheaths part of the pool. This could be on the Upper Hudson, perhaps near Warrensburg.

A lumberman's home was hardly living in the lap of luxury. Scene above, snapped before a Forest Preserve became reality, shows primitive conditions under which lumberjacks lived, sometimes for months at a time.

No chain saws existed in the early days. Trees were felled by use of a cross-cut saw and sawed into logs. Toppings, that is, unused portions, were left to rot in the forest — if, at first fire did not devour the area. And fire often did.

Occasionally a lumber camp was blessed with female presence. The ladies could have been wives who refused to leave husbands who held supervisory posts, visitors – or cooks. A rough life but these two seem to have brought along their "Sunday best" to wear for the occasion of the photograph. Below: Loggers using river boats on the Ausable; exact area unknown. Drownings in this type of work, which often brought the men into whitewater, were not uncommon. If without family, the victim sometimes was buried along the river, with the grave marked by a small wooden cross.

Logs were marked with an emblem chosen by the owner. The mark was inscribed with a "stamping hammer," with the owner's symbol in raised lettering on the surface of the hammer. Thus logs could be separated by owners at the end of long trips down mountain rivers and streams.

Without the faithful horse, logging would have been impossible. They were used to haul and to skid timber – placed in neat piles, ready for loading.

174

"Caught napping" is the title of this photo, obviously posed for the photographer around the turn of the century. In actuality there was very little gold-bricking on the job; the work was hard, the hours long, supervision strict. The gentleman rests alongside a trough through which water is flushed — and logs float to a waiting stream or river.

Chained to low, flat bed sleds, and pulled by a team of patient horses, the logs could be transported to stream and river shorelines, ready to be dumped into the waters for floating downstream. Or, if sawmills were nearby, the timber was transported to the waiting mill. Various and ingenious devices were created to prevent the sled from overtaking the horses on downhill runs — but accidents did happen and animals were crushed under tons of raw lumber.

Called "terminal's end," this photo, taken many years ago and reproduced from an old Fish and Game Commission report, shows pulp logs cascading from a trough into the Ausable River. They were channeled from a distance above and the river carried them to their ultimate destination.

A blackened landscape, victim of a devouring fire. It could very well illustrate the aftermath of a conflagration which is considered among the most destructive in New York State history — the fire which destroyed Long Lake West in September, 1903. More than 450,000 acres were consumed; the fire ate every building in its path and sent residents fleeing for their lives.

"Venison for supper" reads the title. Another drawing from early Fish and Game Commission annual reports. Many of the reports were bound volumes: furnish much material for the writer who delves into history.

Guides and those who paid the freight often became close friends and a good guide was worth his weight in venison any day of the week. "A friendly chat between sportsman and guide" is an apt title.

When the Forest Preserve was created it proved a bonanza for surveyors because lines had to be reestablished and positive boundaries drawn. Even today some lines are open to court action.

"Anglers' camp in the forest – discussing the catch." That's the title of this Watson work of art, shown as are others printed in this volume, in early Fish and Game Commission reports.

The title of this Watson drawing: "Thousand Islands, St. Lawrence River – a maskalonge hooked and coming to gaff." Apparently that was one spelling of muskellunge which, in turn, is another way of spelling the name of the fish!

Another common scene of days gone by and the present — having wet boots pulled by a friendly boot puller, a scene of the past duplicated during the present. Painting by Watson.

Dramatic photo taken of a contestant during White Water Derby races. The 25th annual competition was held in 1982 with the usual audience of thousands. It is interesting to note that while techniques remain the same, there have been big changes during the first race and the 1982 contests. One instance in the financial field: In 1957 when the Derby began, the sum of $13,500 would purchase a three bedroom cottage, with fireplace, porch and sixty feet of frontage on Lake George at Pilot Knob! Things have changed indeed, but the races still call for skill and courage; the Upper Hudson at North Creek and North River has not lost its punch.

See following page for some of those who have figured prominently in administration of the derby.

Clockwise, starting at left: Tim Garrity, co-chairman, and Dr. N.W. Baroudi, entertainment committee chairman, check results during the '82 races; Judge Ken Bennett, among those who gave valuable assistance in instituting the contests and thus adding to the fame of North Creek; George Gardner, left, Editor of the North Creek News-Enterprise, and Bill Carpenter, who did commentary in the past and who now lives in Hawaii; Don Pierson, co-chairman, presents award, with Lloyd Burch, awards chairman, in foreground.

Among the many who have helped preserve North Country identity and ideals and a man who has contributed a great deal in the way of community service in the Lake Pleasant-Speculator-Piseco area, is John Knox. Knox, pictured at right, is shown with the late U.S. Representative Bernard W. (Pat) Kearney, a Fulton County and Adirondack resident. Recognition of the highest sort came to Knox in 1982 when the Adirondack Conservation Council awarded him its Distinguished Conservationist of the Year Award.

Prof. Tom Kelly of Schenectady, a member of the faculty of Siena College, Loudonville, deserves recognition for his efforts in establishing the Adirondack Forum held at the college. Kelly is pictured at the WGY microphone during an interview with Bob Cudmore of the well known "Contact" program. The Siena man is considered an authority on the Adirondacks.

Accidents do happen and this photo proves it. It represents what happens when boat meets shore — or, putting it another way, when shore meets boat. Incidents such as this are not too rare in the Lake George area of The Narrows where islands are close and channels difficult to negotiate unless one has experience as a guide. Photo by Walter Grishkot.

A man of the past. Decades ago the author photographed a beloved resident of the Lake George region, Al Merrick, former printer, former editor of the Lake George Mirror who, upon retiring, lived in a small "cottage" at the eastern end of Beach Road. He often visited Sky Harbor, then run by George McGowan of Lake George, and there partook of his favorite concoction – a glass of beer into which he poured a jigger of gin. Merrick often played Santa for the village and provided an able characterization indeed. He has been long gone.

In the late 1800's you hauled yourself up Prospect Mt. at Lake George by foot — or, if you had the animal, by horse. But there was another method — climbing to 2,600 feet above sea level by the Otis Incline Railway. This unusual photo, used through courtesy of the Lake George Historical Society, looks down at two cable cars which have just completed using sidings to pass each other. Otis Engineering and Construction Company took six months to build the project and at the time it was the longest cable railroad in the United States.

Distance was one and two-fifths miles; trains ran every half hour and the fare was a whopping fifty cents, round trip. Refreshments were served at the "Club House" on top the peak. This photo probably snapped about 1897. Today, of course, a memorial highway reaches top and bottom. Part of the cable machinery still exists at the top.

Amazing is Oto, nine-year-old champion black Persian cat owned by Grace Hudowalski of Schroon Lake and Albany. Reason: Annually Oto tosses a social event and sale of stationery for benefit of the Schroon-North Hudson Historical Society. The super-salescatlady raised $231 this year and this, added to previous years, amounts to a total of $2,000! Of course, humans have something to do about it all, but Oto supervises. Her owner is executive secretary of the Adirondack Association. Party and sale held on the East side of Schroon Lake.

Above oddity: Money pouch made of tanned beaver tail. Far left: Dried castoreum pouches from beaver, sometimes known as "barkstone" or "beaver castors." Glands believed to have medicinal value. Center photo: An Adirondacker with a sense of humor, if not history, erected this sign, self-explanatory, in the Keene Valley area!

The author is highly indebted to the late Walter J. Schoonmaker for several of the wildlife photographs reproduced in this volume. "Schoonie," a personal friend, studied vertebrate zoology at Cornell University and art at Syracuse and the University of Valencia, Spain. He served on the professional staff of the New York State Museum for thirty-five years as an assistant zoologist and later as museum exhibit planner. Above photo taken in his earlier years as he completed a snowshoe trip to inspect a beaver lodge.

Thanks to:

Without friends, without individuals expert in their fields, an author is apt to flounder like a trout on a mudbank. All of which leads into the fact that this writer is indebted enormously to many individuals who shared their expertise and many organizations which cheerfully offered research facilities in the writing of this volume.

My thanks, therefore, to the following:

Dick Case, Syracuse newspaper columnist for much of the factual background in the Roxalana Druse execution; John La Duke, Saranac Lake photographer; Arnold LeFevre, Director, Capital Newspapers Photographic Department, for photos taken at the Adirondack Museum; Skip Dickstein and Fred McKinney, Capital Newspapers photographers for valuable contributions; Walt Grishkot, photographer, long time friend and originator of the Adirondack Balloon Festival; Mrs. Suye Gambino, voluntary caretaker, and Susanne Whitcomb, guide, at the Grant Cottage.

Also: Don Fangboner, Lake George Historical Association; Charles Hawley, Chairman, Lake George Park Commission; Robert Hall, Willsboro, former Editor, Conservationist Magazine; Bill Roden, well-known North Country columnist; William Crowley, Adirondack Museum; Prof. Tom Kelly, Siena College, sparkplug of the Adirondack Forum; New York State Police, Troop B, Ray Brook, for photos of abused horses; Robert O'Brien, Niagara Mohawk Power Corp. for assistance in preparing the Sacandaga Reservoir chapter; Assemblyman Neil Kelleher, Troy; Alice Clements, Philadelphia, for her remarkable chipmunk picture; Peter Brownsey, Niskayuna, for the privilege of using his Rockwell Falls and D&H Railroad bridge photos.

Also: Dr. Edward Becker, Albany area veterinarian; George McGowan, Lake George; P.F. Loope, former Executive Secretary, Adirondack Mountain Club; Ted Aber, Hamilton County Historian; Peter Nye of EnCon's Endangered Species unit and others within his department; the late Walter Schoonmaker, a friend of yesteryear, for many animal photos used herein; personnel at EnCon's Wildlife Resources Center, Delmar; Conservationist Magazine; Clayt Seagears, artist and retired Director of the Division of Conservation Education and the New York State Department of Commerce.

Also: Herkimer County Historical Society; Adirondack Museum, Blue Mt. Lake; New York State Museum, New York State Library and the Clinton County Historical Society.

My sincere regrets if I have ignored anyone who assisted. Any omission is inadvertent.